FROM THE VOID TO THE THRONE

Shadow to Substance

PAUL G. SAMES

WestBow
PRESS
A DIVISION OF THOMAS NELSON

WestBow Press books may be ordered through booksellers or by contacting:

WestBow Press
A Division of Thomas Nelson
1663 Liberty Drive
Bloomington, IN 47403
www.westbowpress.com
1-(866) 928-1240

ISBN: 978-1-4908-0010-3 (sc)
ISBN: 978-1-4908-0011-0 (hc)
ISBN: 978-1-4908-0009-7 (e)

Library of Congress Control Number: 2013911888

Printed in the United States of America.

WestBow Press rev. date: 8/6/2013

"Scripture quotations taken from the Amplified® Bible,
Copyright © 1954, 1958, 1962, 1964, 1965, 1987 by The Lockman Foundation
Used by permission." (www.Lockman.org)

"Scripture taken from The Message. Copyright © 1993, 1994, 1995, 1996,
2000, 2001, 2002. Used by permission of NavPress Publishing Group."

Other quotes are from NASB and KJV Bible translations. (public domain)

Chapter 1 (Part 1)

THE SEEDS OF LIFE SOWN!

Many people in life are desperately searching for the answer that will bring fulfillment and purpose and are asking the age old questions:

How did I get here?

What is the purpose of this earth walk?

What happens at death?

All of the world's major religions grapple with these questions and attempt to bring adequate answers. For many years I studied world religions, as well as occult, Para psychological and philosophical phenomena. This resulted in much knowledge but did not set me free with love and truth (knowledge puffs up but love edifies). At the time, I was convinced that the paths I had chosen were the paths of life, because I did have many and varied supernatural experiences, some of which were incredibly beautiful.

The spiritual melting pot that boiled over in the 1960s had a powerful impact on my life. I was fascinated by the whole spiritual/philosophical thrust made popular by the Beatles, Timothy Leary, Eastern religious gurus and many others. I became fascinated with Eastern philosophies, new age spiritualism and experimentation with psychedelic drugs, as did many of my contemporaries. The psychedelic experiences totally altered my perception of the universe and without even realizing it; I started embracing a Buddhist/Hinduistic cosmology. I almost instantaneously developed an insatiable spiritual appetite for all kinds of cosmic theories. This seemed wonderful and I was convinced I had found reality and truth.

In late 1973, my brother Roger returned to Sydney, Australia, after living in Canada and the U.S. for 7 years. He had been recently living in Oahu, Hawaii for some time and had also been involved in a spiritual odyssey, which led him into yogic teachings from the East. At times Roger would write me, informing me of his latest spiritual discovery, or cosmic revelation. I would relish these letters as profound moments, as I also was on a voyage for spiritual discovery, so to speak. Rogers letters would at times contain impressive Eastern spiritual terminology, such as karma, satori, yoga, etc., and many other Indian terms, to describe different Eastern religious experiences or principles. All this was received with deep appreciation and approval.

One day in late 1973, I received a letter from Roger with a dramatic and radically different message. At first it shocked and rocked me to my foundations and then it angered me. The very opening line said, "Jesus Christ defeated Satan 2000 years ago at Calvary when He died and rose again, thereby stripping Satan of the keys of death and hell. Hallelujah!" I could not believe what I was reading. To me, at that time, this was a total sellout to the establishment forces of conservative western politics and religious culture. I was deeply incensed to say the least and threw the letter down in disappointment and disgust. I felt betrayed and made a resolve to avoid Roger and his letters. Amazingly, he returned to Australia a few weeks after his letter was received.

Just prior to Christmas 1973 Roger returned to Australia and spontaneously, I encountered him in my Mothers apartment. I saw he looked different; his face had a peaceful glow about it that was different to the acid inspired effulgence, of many of my contemporaries. I was challenged and somehow weakened, and got out of his presence as soon as possible. At that time I believed that all religions or spiritual paths, led to the same One God or enlightenment.

I did not so much mind someone making Jesus Christ their guru or spiritual master, though even this, in my estimation was inferior, because any Christian path, according to Timothy Leary (the 60s trip guru who had become the chief luminary in my particular orbit) could only hope to bring one to level 4 or sensory consciousness. Leary said the highest consciousness was what he termed level 1 or atomic/electronic consciousness. His theory claimed that this state was attained only by the most enlightened Buddhist monks, or the highest strata of psychedelic researchers on large doses of hallucinogens. At level 1 the whole physical world (Oneself included), dissolved into shimmering latticework's of energy patterns and one had the experience of "The White Light of the Void" or Nirvana.

Anyway back to the story, the thing that really irritated me about my brother Roger was that he was declaring that Jesus Christ was the "ONLY WAY". This was a powerful affront to my New Age, cosmic/universalist belief system. I was therefore determined to prove that "my god was as good as his God" or that my light was as bright as or brighter than his Light. I did my best to convey my universalistic spiritual knowledge to him. I hoped I would be able to dazzle my brother with a concoction of contemporary cosmology. I reasoned to myself that I would present my Eastern spirituality with such eloquence that his Jesus Freak teachings would collapse into foolish irrelevance. My mission was to bring him out of his delusion and into my perceived "realities of cosmic consciousness." We had a Roman Catholic upbringing, so I thought maybe he had just reverted to childhood conditioning and become an overgrown altar boy. Little did I realize how in fact blind and deceived I was.

Prior to returning to Oz, my brother had been involved, after his conversion to Jesus Christ, with a Christian fellowship called "The Lighthouse". Many of its members had been converted out of former lifestyles of drug use and alternative philosophies. This church had really learnt how to pray and Roger had them praying for me to find Jesus Christ. Anyway let me explain what happened. In January 1974, I was at a party at Tamarama Beach in Sydney, Australia. This was a wild and crazy affair; there were copious quantities of champagne, marijuana and psychedelics being consumed by the participants. We were all dressed in swimming attire and I initially, was having a wonderful time, until, suddenly (in one split second) I was aware of my own undone and wasted condition. Instantly, I saw that my whole life and existence up until that point had been a total waste, an exercise in futility. All at once the party lost its appeal. In fact I was repelled and I ran away by myself, to a secluded part of the beach. As I ran, I became aware of someone or something pursuing me. At first I thought it was maybe the police, as I had been flaunting drugs at the party. Also my stereo speaker cabinets at home were stuffed full of cannabis.

Suddenly, I realized that whatever was chasing me was not physical; it was of a spiritual unseen nature. At this point in my life I did not believe in a personal being called God or a personal being of evil called Satan (or in demons or evil spirits). My concept of God and the devil was of impersonal spiritual forces that influence our attitudes and action. I thought that the being named Satan, in the Bible, was nothing more than a mythological creature. I was now in for a rude wakening. Now, unexpectedly, I had the dreadful revelation that spiritual beings without bodies were in hot pursuit. I fell under a tree and realized that with my eyes open or shut I was seeing the same scene. Grotesque figures moved in martial arts style configuration before my eyes. They had horrible countenances with bugged out eyes, fanglike teeth and flames for hair. They were living testimony to the statues of gods or demons one sees in places like Bali, Indonesia. It was a shocking revelation, to realize these idols are representations of real living spirit beings, in the unseen (to the natural eye) spiritual realm. It dawned on me that there were real spiritual beings that these statues depicted. These beings were not loving, compassionate or merciful in any way. These demons were also superhuman and powerful, no person of flesh and blood could hope to overcome their strength, without the help and authority of the One True God.

The atmosphere was filled with malevolence; it was quite simply your worst nightmare come true. The whole atmosphere seemed to be thick and heavy with tangible evil and darkness. I was desperately grasping for some area of knowledge or expertise, which would remove me from this horrific world. Often, people in critical and life threatening situations speak of their whole life flashing before their eyes, almost instantaneously. Well, this is exactly what happened to me. Every talent, knowledge, skill and belief I possessed flashed up before me but seemed to melt in impotent uselessness in relation to the crisis confronting me. All the spiritual research, I had sown so much time into, now was powerless to deliver me. In fact, I became aware that the spiritual entities, which were now so vehemently threatening me, had in fact been the source of the spiritual revelations I had trusted and believed. It almost seemed that the demons sneered at my naïve foolishness.

I am convinced that my whole eternal future was at stake in this dilemma. I was cornered by spiritual beings vastly more powerful and intelligent than myself. Indeed my position seemed hopeless, in the face of such spiritual firepower arrayed against me. I was filled with terror and despair, there was no escape. I felt I was the helpless prey, with the demons closing in for the eternal kill, so to speak.

Just at the point where all seemed lost and there seemed absolutely no hope, an amazing and magnificent, miraculous intervention occurred.

For some unknown reason, The Name of Jesus, exploded out of my mouth and spirit with overwhelming, dynamic force, It was like a space shuttle burning rocket fuel, developing escape velocity and thrust at Cape Canaveral, I know that sounds facetious to some but it was such an explosive and intense utterance. It was as though every fibre of my spirit, soul and body proclaimed His Name. It was not just an oral proclamation. It was massively authoritative and it came not out of my head or my mind but right out of my heart. My mental processes were not involved with what took place; God bypassed the old brain or grey matter and revealed Himself directly to my spirit man, what the Bible calls "THE HIDDEN MAN OF THE HEART". (1 Peter 3:4) Some may now be saying, "Surely God would not lobotomize someone", that is absolutely true, God created the mind and intellect for His Glory but there are realms of direct spiritual experience, where the Holy Spirit will totally bypass the mental computer and manifest Himself directly to the spirit of the individual.. Remember, we are a spirit, we have a mind but we live in a body. Paul expounds this truth, in relation to the area of praying in the spirit below.

1 Corinthians 14:13-15.

"FOR IF I PRAY IN A TONGUE MY SPIRIT PRAYS BUT MY MIND IS UNFRUITFUL. SO WHAT SHALL I DO? I WILL PRAY WITH MY SPIRIT, BUT

I WILL ALSO PRAY WITH MY MIND. I WILL SING WITH MY SPIRIT, BUT I WILL ALSO SING WITH MY MIND."
King James Version

I know in my particular case, it was Gods chosen method to bypass my chatterbox mind and flood my spirit, with pure love and dynamic Power. In retrospect, I can appreciate His wisdom, as my mind was absolutely steeped in eastern mysticism, and cosmic philosophy. I prided myself in Zen humor and Taoist dualism. This meant that I perceived the entire universe as one huge cosmic joke and that everything was the same anyway, i.e. all paths eventually wind up in the same place. I saw evil as containing good (dualism) and good containing evil. Mentally, I was a slippery one to pin down with the Gospel; my mind was steeped in a myriad of cosmic refutations. I was truly a spiritual chameleon. The reptile called a chameleon is able to change his colors to match his surrounding. I changed my beliefs according to my company, as this philosophy claims to embrace all belief systems.

1 Corinthians 2:14 [14] But [a]a natural man does not accept the things of the Spirit of God, for they are foolishness to him; and he cannot understand them, because they are spiritually [b]appraised. (NASB)

Personally, I believe I was so deceived and had my mind programmed with so many spiritual beliefs that the only way for God to reach me, was by this massive manifestation of His Person and Reality to my spirit, this by far superseded any other spiritual experience I have ever had. Thank God for His Mercy! (Actually dear reader, it is a far greater testimony, to be able to say that one had become a Christian at age 5 and had never strayed from the courts of the Lord, than to be rescued as an adult.)

The Bible and Jesus Himself make it abundantly clear that the faith of Abraham (faith that does not require sight) is a far more blessed thing than the faith of Thomas (faith that demands evidence).

Jesus SAID TO DOUBTING THOMAS IN

John 20:2 (NASB)

[29] Jesus *said to him, "Because you have seen Me, have you believed? Blessed *are* they who did not see, and *yet* believed."

Chapter 2

EXPLOSION OF LIGHT

Suffice it to say, at the sound of that Name of Jesus, there was a massive and glorious explosion of Gods life and Love and Power. Instantly, there was a total and stupendous release from the power and presence of the demon spirits. They left as quickly as the darkness leaves, when a powerful light is switched on in a dark room. It was just "zap" and the Love and Light of Jesus Christ permeated every part of my world. I started weeping and sobbing, right out of the innermost depths of my being. With each sob, it seemed that a great wave of liquid fiery love and light, would course through my very bone marrow. My emotions and mind were also injected with a deep impartation of Divine healing and freedom from the many hurts and sorrows, that life had dealt me. It was totally and absolutely awesome, in the deepest and truest meaning of the word. Thank God for His Supernatural Divine intervention. I knew that I had met the Living God; this was not the mere embracing of a set of rules, commandments or doctrines. This was a Spiritual "heart" collision with the Risen Christ.

Hebrews 7:16 [16] Who is made, not after the law of a carnal commandment, but after the power of an endless life. (KJV)

Yes, indeed this was more than mental assent to a written code, on tablets of stone or paper and ink. This was a life altering, regenerating, converting encounter with the Living Word Himself, even Jesus Christ of Nazareth the Son of the Living God. Please, don't misunderstand me, I am not invalidating the extreme importance of the Written Word of Scripture, even Our Lord Jesus quoted Scripture. "IT IS WRITTEN", He said, when He counterattacked Satan's temptations. Without a deep and ongoing study and knowledge of the Bible, we are like sailors in the midst of a vast ocean without map or compass.

15 Be diligent to present yourself approved to God as a workman who does not need to be ashamed, accurately handling the word of truth. 2 Timothy 2:1 (NASB)

One must never forget that there is a universe of difference between mental assent or intellectual agreement and life changing heart revelation of Biblical Truth. The Bible says even the "devils believe and tremble" but never have saving faith. This is why James said faith without works are dead (James 2:16-26 KJV). The Apostle Paul says:

15 But when God, who had set me apart *even* from my mother's womb and called me through His grace, was pleased 16 to reveal His Son in me so that I might preach Him among the Gentiles, I did not immediately consult with [a]flesh and blood, Galatians 1:15-16 (NASB)

God, by operation of the Person of the Holy Spirit, must reveal His Son to our inner man or spirit in order for the New Birth to be executed.

True Christianity produces the fruit of the Spirit through revelation knowledge of the Word in ones life. Pseudo intellectual religiosity, produces only doctrinal arguments, through information knowledge. True Biblical intellectual belief includes not just head knowledge of doctrine but Heart Revelation by the Holy Spirit. The Spirit and the Word are one; they are not opposed to each other. An old Christian saying and Scriptural truth is: "If you are all Word you dry up, if you are all Spirit you blow up. If you are a mixture of both you grow up." A gun cartridge with gunpowder and no lead, will make a loud bang, but will not penetrate a target. A cartridge with only the lead projectile and no gunpowder is equally impotent. We need the gunpowder of the Spirit and the lead of the written Word, to speak metaphorically. The Word will then reach men's hearts with life giving velocity and impact. God is calling us in these last days to TRANSFORMING REVELATION KNOWLEDGE IN CHRIST not to RELIGIOUS DOCTRINAL ARGUMENTS OF LEGALISM.

The power of God hit and unalterably changed me forever. I knew instantly that I must go home and dispose of my drug supply. I headed for home, to get rid of the marijuana I had hidden inside the stereo speaker. I was so filled with the Fire of God, that I kept saying to myself constantly "JESUS CHRIST HAS BAPTIZED ME IN FIRE!" What made this extraordinary was the fact that to the best of my knowledge, I had never read this anywhere; it was just such a deep inner realization. I was so excited and flooded with the zeal of God, that I just started walking up to people and would urge them to forget any other god and give their life to Jesus.

I felt like was an unquenchable fireball for Jesus Christ. On the way, I stopped by the apartment of one of my closest friends, Karel. His life was absolutely steeped in occult research. I knocked on his front door. When he opened to me at 2 a.m. in a haze of drugs and sleep I boldly proclaimed with missionary fire, "I have found Jesus Christ. I've been baptized in the fire of Jesus Christ, nothing else matters now, only Jesus Christ." He hurriedly shut the door in shock. It was an amazing experience, I sensed that my whole being was burning with Fire and shining with Light. I knew that as people looked at my face they could see the Oil of Joy and Gods Glory, shining on my face.

8 Who is like the wise man and who knows the interpretation of a matter? A man's wisdom illumines [a]him and causes his stern face to beam. Ecc 8:1 (NASB)

15 And fixing their gaze on him, all who were sitting in the [a]Council saw his face like the face of an angel Acts 6:15 (NASB) (about Stephen the evangelist)

I could not contain myself; I knew that I must tell everyone of this encounter with Jesus. I decided I would go and see another friend named Dave. He was involved in very dark occult practices, things like Black magic, dark metal music, witchcraft and Satanism. As he opened the door, I boldly proclaimed Jesus to him. I think I probably came across like Charlton Heston, playing Moses in the great Cecil B. De Mille Biblical epic. In spite of what may have appeared, to the casual observer, as my theatrical extravagance, I was absolutely sincere about my born again/ baptism in fire experience. My friend reeled back in shock and horror, not unlike a vampire when confronted with a cross in the movies. I recall him saying, "There's a light coming off you"! As he shielded his eyes and shut the door on me. I also ran into my cousin Jeff Kennedy, who had been at the original party at the beach. He had a bottle of champagne in his hand, which he was drinking and he was also smoking a marijuana joint.

I started telling him what had happened to me at the beach and he told me he too had received a powerful experience with Jesus, a few days previously, while speaking with my brother Roger. He instantly threw the champagne and marijuana in to a trash can and started to praise the Name of Jesus.

We then decided to find a dope party that had been planned at an address in Bondi Junction, about 5 miles from the beach where I had the encounter with Jesus. We decided we were going to tell everyone at the party, about our "Close encounters of the God Kind". It was now about 12 midnight! I was so excited about Jesus, that I completely forgot I was only wearing swimming shorts. I walked off with Jeff to Bondi Junction in the middle of the night, to find this dope party so we could tell them about Jesus. On the way we told every person we saw about Jesus and what happened to me that night. I couldn't help myself. It was the most wonderful thing that had ever happened to me and I was not about to keep it to myself. We searched all over but could not find the party, so we started walking down the main street of Bondi Junction and telling everyone we saw about Jesus. Here it was about 1 a.m. and I'm still in my swim shorts, now miles from the beach in a major shopping area, proclaiming Jesus to all and sundry, with great joy and zeal.

Chapter 3

THE LAW GIVES GRACE

A passing police car noticed me and pulled over to question us on our unusual behavior. This was a tremendous experience for me. I had been paranoid of the police, as they had represented opposition forces to me, so to speak. Now as I looked at these two officers, I realized they were on my side. I knew I was no longer an outlaw and had nothing to fear. I experienced a deep inner realization that the police are ordained of God for social protection. This again was totally from the Holy Spirit as I had never read ROMANS 13:3-4

Romans 13:3 (NASB)

3 For rulers are not a cause of fear for [a]good behavior, but for evil. Do you want to have no fear of authority? Do what is good and you will have praise from the same; 4 for it is a minister of God to you for good. But if you do what is evil, be afraid; for it does not bear the sword for nothing; for it is a minister of God, an avenger who brings wrath on the one who practices evil.

As the policemen approached, I said to them with a beatific smile on my face "JESUS LOVES YOU." They both just looked at me with wonderful smiles on their faces and one just said "IT'S COOL". Then they turned away and got in their car, full of joy and peace. This was a major sign of God to me, as I had never seen police act like this before. They had always been tough and aggressive in my previous encounters. At this point I realized I still had not made it home to dispose of the pound of marijuana in my stereo cabinet. I had just been distracted by many missions on the way. Now I turned walking full speed for home. It was about 5 miles and I walked rejoicing all the way. As soon as I got there, I tried to stuff all the dope down the toilet and flush it but it blocked all the plumbing. After some quick plumbing maneuvers, I retrieved most of it. Now dripping wet, I decided to take it to the cliff top near the back of my apartment and throw it in the sea. I called a friend of mine named Mick and told him of my experience with Christ (he had been influenced by my brother Rogers Bible talks too), he told me he had some marijuana as well, so I said bring it over and he did and we threw it off the Dover Heights cliffs together. WHAT A GLORIOUS TIME!

I awoke the very next morning after a few hours sleep, I was not nearly as zealous and excited as the previous night but I knew that I was no longer the same person and never would be again. I decided to call my brother Roger and tell him what happened. He listened in stunned amazement and when I finished my recount of the previous night, there was silence for quite a long time. Looking back, he probably was wondering if I was crazy, or just mocking him with a fictional story, so I could laugh at him. After all, it was an extravagant testimony. It probably sounded too good to be true. After what seemed an interminable period of time he exclaimed "WHAT A VICTORY!" He was stunned by the rapid and exorbitant answer to his prayers. This was a huge affirmation to Roger, about the Power of Prayer. He had the whole Lighthouse Church in Hawaii praying for me. This was gigantic. In fact, it was Rogers's ministry that instigated the salvation of both myself and my circle of friends. Roger went to Heaven in 1991 but his spiritual legacy still works here on earth.

I decided to go down to the beach where this had all happened. It was a beautiful Australian summer day and the beach was packed. All of my friends were down there, surf gurus, beach philosophers, drug users and dealers, pretty girls, you name it. I just naturally assumed that they would all be clamoring to hear of my conversion and encounter with Jesus. In the past, they had always been interested, when I talked about my non-Christian spiritual experiences. How wrong I was now! I was met by a solid wall of resistance and disdain! Some openly mocked me; one claimed I had blown a gasket in my cerebral circuits. When one asked me for some marijuana, I told them all I had thrown my dope into the sea. This really "set the cat amongst the pigeons" so to speak. In their estimation, this was the height of madness, throwing quantities of extremely expensive top quality grass away. This was not just economic and social suicide, but to the hippy set I ran with it was like blasphemy. "That does it," said one guy. "You are a total idiot! You have finally flipped." "HALLELUJAH! PRAISE THE LORD!" I said. One sarcastically responded with, "Hallelujah! That'll do ya."

I was ostracized by the majority of my former associates. They now decided to take attitudes that ranged from mockery and hostility, to piteous patronizing. "Well, you are weak and need a crutch Paul; maybe an authority figure like Christ is just what will help you! Obviously this is what you need." Yet, the mocking rejection did not discourage me. I could not help but preach Jesus everywhere I went and I would go down to the beach daily for weeks after my conversion and would speak of Jesus to anyone who would listen. I would also take down tracts and Christian publications my brother had given me and distribute them amongst the young people.

Chapter 4

CHRISTIANS NOT PERFECT?

We found out about some Christian meetings, which sounded exciting. Now to say you were going to a meeting was no problem to my psyche, as it did not sound alarms in my head like the word "church". My concept at that time of church was of a building or man made organization and it conjured up some memories from my denominational childhood that were a stumbling block to my thinking.

So we went to a Christian group, which used the word "centre" rather than church, which was no problem to me. (Many churches in the 70s and 80s used the word centre rather than church) This was a powerful church on the North Shore of Sydney, which flowed freely in the gifts and power of God. I received some wonderful teaching and grounding in the Word of God. I talked to the pastor about moving into a big ministry type house that quite a few lived in who attended the church. He agreed that it would be good for my spiritual development. In fact, the pastor himself lived there.

All was smooth the first few months I lived in the house, until I started having problems with the middle class cultural aspects of the church. I had come out of a hippie mentality and at this stage, I had no understanding of the fact that God desires to prosper His servants, even materially.

I started judging the pastor in my heart for driving a fancy car, which was given to him as a gift by a car dealer in his congregation. I also started feeling as if I would be turned into a corny clone if I stayed in the church. I can now see that Satan was doing a real job on my mind, so to speak. The devil started to really use some of the rebellion that was still in my heart, to drive me out of fellowship. Now to be honest, this church did have some problems that finally caused a financial controversy to erupt, resulting in the pastor resigning and the church going into a major decline. (In fact, it doesn't exist today but most of the former members have gone on to serve God in other churches)

But, I left fellowship freely and do not place the blame on this particular church, or on the pastor, who is a wonderful man of God, who has gone on to do great missionary exploits.

Chapter 5

FALLING FROM GRACE

When I left the church, I did not want to leave Jesus or the faith but I was now left without fellowship. Roger also had been disillusioned by the church. He had gone north to another city. I drifted back among my old friends. One old friend of mine, who I started visiting, had become a major importer of hashish into Sydney. One day he had reluctantly received as part payment for some hashish, a quantity of heroin. I found myself spending most of my time at this friends place. I did not want to smoke pot any more; it only made me feel paranoid. Now my friend started smoking this heroin every time I was there and he was urging me to help myself. I did not want to; as I knew it was a dark and dangerous drug. Finally, I gave in to the temptation and was ushered into the vacuum like counterfeit of peace that heroin affords. I liked it; it seemed to silence my nagging conscience, which constantly troubled me since I had dropped out of Christian fellowship.

I spent all my time with my cohort/friend who now was giving me as much free smack as I wanted. We would sit at a table in his bedroom with the windows covered with black blankets, to keep the light out and simulate a constant night. The bedside table would be set with heroin and other substances. I quickly developed a physical addiction, without even realizing it was happening to me. Someone once said "The downward spiral of narcotics is so well oiled by the drug itself that you don't even suspect you are going down until you hit rock bottom."

You might be saying." How could one who had such a profound experience with Jesus, now be in such abominable sin and darkness? Let me say this, my intention was never to escape from Christ but to escape from a religious structure that I perceived to be wanting to clone me in a "cookie cutter" pattern. I wanted Jesus but I could not understand why being a Christian, meant one must "wear a tie" and conform to middle class fashions and cultural traditions. I also now recognize that I did have underlying rebellion and immaturity, which gave me some added complications in the situation. I believe that given grace and time the Holy Spirit would have changed my externals, such as dress, etc., as indeed He of course has; now it's almost 40 years later.

I think that by placing an undue emphasis on dress codes and externals, etc., the church placed a pressure of restriction on me that prompted me to throw the baby out with the bathwater, as it were.

If I had been a more mature Christian, I would not have reacted so radically and would have used more wisdom. Being a baby Christian, I rejected the whole church structure and found no place of nurturing to return to, seeing my brother had left the area and was not doing too well himself. Today, I own a number of suits and enjoy dressing respectably for the appropriate occasions. But I fully realize that a Christian is just as anointed in a pair of Levi's and a sweat shirt, as he is in a 3 piece suit with Italian shoes! Both fashion statements are equally appropriate within their respective contexts.

After all, the anointing does not proceed from your Gucci tie but from the Holy Spirit. Anyway, back to the testimony.

Having said all that, the bottom line is this. I was to blame for my own devastating backslide, no one else. I cannot "pass the buck" and blame any church or pastor. I was the one who blew it. In fact, the original church I attended in 1974 helped me in many ways. Even today, I recall the great times of blessing I received there.

I became a drug addled mess, yet, in the midst of all this, I knew that Jesus was the only way out. It was weird, my drug oriented lifestyle denied Christ but if the situation demanded it, I would still confess Him with my mouth and even witness His Reality and love to others. It was a classic case of my Spirit being willing but my flesh being weak (Jesus, Matthew 26:41).

Once I was at a wild party, where everyone was bombed on drugs of one description or another. A truly good friend of mine was on LSD and I was nodding out in the corner, on narcotics. There was also a warlock there (male witch) on LSD, as well. My friend started discussing spiritual philosophies with him. This warlock became aggressively outspoken concerning his Satanist beliefs and was really starting to afflict my friend with torment and fear. Suddenly, the Power of the Holy Spirit was all over me like Fire, and I was instantly free of all narcotic effects. I felt a bit like Elijah taking on the prophets of Baal (I Kings 18:19-40). I confronted the warlock and proclaimed Jesus Christ as King and Lord over all satanic power. The poor fellow backed off, like a whipped pup with his tail between his legs. I turned to the guy having the bad LSD trip and asked him to give his life to Christ. The power of God hit him and he started weeping. The drug effects were broken and I led him in the salvation prayer. He was filled with joy and wanted to know more, but as quick as it had left, the narcosis came back on me, as the anointing waned. I said to my friend, "Don't ask me! I'm a backslidden shipwreck. I need repentance and forgiveness more than you. I'm a mess. You need to find a good pastor to help you." Some are now saying. "God wouldn't use someone in that condition. The Holy Spirit is Holy! He would not anoint a druggo." Well, he anointed a donkey once (Numbers 22:30) to prophesy and He still sometimes speaks through donkeys or turkeys like us today. We must realize that the anointing is no indication of ones character or personal holiness. If there are no sanctified saints available to use, God will use even the worst backslider to reach a lost soul! Sounds outrageous I know but even recent church history has many stories of drunken, immoral preachers, who sometimes led great revivals.

Romans 11:29 (NASB)

^{29} for the gifts and the calling of God are irrevocable.

Willing in Spirit/Weak in Flesh

I would regularly read the Bible, even in my fallen condition, and would even love to hold impromptu Bible studies if someone showed an interest. I had one good friend named Grant who would love to hear me reading aloud the Bible. We would take drugs together and when we were feeling good he would ask me to read the Bible to him. Once he injected some super pure heroin and clinically died right in front of me. He hit the kitchen floor, lifeless and purple before he could even remove the syringe from his vein. His eyes were rolled back in his head and I could detect no pulse or heartbeat. I slapped him on the face - no response. I threw cold water over him; I applied heart massage - nothing. Then in heartbreak and weeping desperation I threw myself across his lifeless body and called on the love and mercy of God in Jesus Name to give him another chance, he was only 19 at the time. Instantly, he responded and miraculously recovered and rose up and went down to Tamarama Beach surfing 20 minutes later. (He was an awesome surfer) He gave thanks to Jesus but didn't even realize, at the time, that he had been clinically dead for several minutes until Jesus revived him. The amazing thing was he overdosed again like this and again was miraculously revived by prayer.

I promised God to break free of the addiction and serve Him, but the iron chains of bondage did not easily yield. Oftentimes I would kneel in front of the TV, after hearing a TV evangelist and ask Gods forgiveness and promise to stay off dope, but 10 minutes later I would find myself leaving the house to purchase drugs. I was in a seemingly hopeless bondage and satan would lie to me and tell me there was no way I could be forgiven as my sins were too deep and dastardly. The Apostle Paul experienced this at a certain point in his Christian experience, he recounts it below. I was having a classic Romans 7 dilemna.

Romans 7:19-21 (NASB)

[19] For the good that I want, I do not do, but I practice the very evil that I do not want. [20] But if I am doing the very thing I do not want, I

am no longer the one doing it, but sin which dwells in me.

[21] I find then the [a]principle that evil is present in me, the one who wants to do good.

[22] For I joyfully concur with the law of God [o] in the inner man, [23] but I see a different law in [p]the members of my body, waging war against the law of my mind and making me a prisoner [q]of the law of sin which is in my members. [24] Wretched man that I am! Who will set me free from [r]the body of this death? [25] Thanks be to God through Jesus Christ our Lord!

ROMANS 8:2 NASB For the law of the Spirit of life [a] in Christ Jesus has set you free from the law of sin and of death

Isaiah 1:18 (NASB)[18] "Come now, and let us reason together,"
Says the LORD,
"Though your sins are as scarlet,

They will be as white as snow;
Though they are red like crimson,
They will be like wool.

My condition and addiction grew steadily worse. At one point, I went to a doctor at my mothers request and he referred me to a psychiatrist. I told this psychiatrist, that he was deluded if he thought he could help me, I informed him that only Jesus Christ could set me free, I rebuked the poor doc for trying to do what only God can do. (The poor doc, he was just doing his job, he just stared at me like a dog with a new dish) Another doctor later told a family friend that in his estimation, I would live only a matter of months because of my prolonged drug binges. I had a very strong constitution and because I was still only very young, I withstood the ordeal quite well considering the magnitude of it. Nevertheless, in January 1977, I was becoming weakened in a big way.

A Mother Hears from the Big Boss

My mother, who was a wonderful Christian, was interceding in prayer for me in a powerful way. She reached a point where she realized, that it would take a Divine Miracle of Great Power, to break me out of what seemed like an inevitable appointment with death any day. She had already once found me convulsing on the floor at the point of death in her apartment. God gave her a word of wisdom and she promised to obey Him. The Lord said to her, "Go and live on the North Coast of New South Wales near Byron Bay and ask Paul to come with you." When she asked me, I said I would. I really wanted to make the break from drugs and I knew in my heart that God was truly in this trip up North. There was a real sense of destiny about it.

The day we left Sydney I purchased some narcotic powder which I reasoned to myself I would use to smoothly and gradually bring myself off the habit. The only problem was I used it totally stupidly and it was consumed in 2 days flat and I was stuck to face a cold turkey situation.

When my mother had become settled in a beachside apartment, I left to go and stay with 2 friends in the tropical hinterland, who were living in an old river side banana packing shed, which they had converted into a residence. They were also growing a crop of marijuana behind their house.

Chapter 6

MIRACLE RECEIVED

After a couple of days of abstinence from the smack, (heroin) I was starting to experience severe withdrawals. I lay on the floor of the the old banana shack in deep depression and mental anguish, my body was aching all over. It was just like the old John Lennon song "Cold Turkey." Insects and bugs (real, not imaginary) crawled all over me and some were biting me. I was so weak and depressed; I had neither the strength nor the inclination to stop them. I had mental images of being trapped in a giant web, with a huge spider closing in on me. I was beyond the stage of panic. It was more like being in giant despairs dungeon, as related in Bunyan's" PILGRIMS PROGRESS". I knew that Jesus was the way out but it seemed I had no faith or ability to believe. I desperately needed a miracle.

God is such a merciful Father and just when we think all is lost; He often intervenes and proves His resurrection Glory again and again. An inner voice as clear as someone speaking in the same room, with authority and incisive penetration, reverberated through my spirit, soul and body. The Holy inner voice seemed to cut through to the very marrow of my being. Hallelujah; I knew it was the Living Word Himself, Jesus Christ of Nazareth. He was speaking the same Creative Words of Life that had created the universe itself. Obviously, He was doing a different work in me than when He said, "LET THERE BE LIGHT" in Genesis, but it was the same Life, the same seed, the same principle. Jesus spoke to me eight simple, yet awesomely life changing words. "I HAVE GIVEN YOU AUTHORITY OVER ALL THIS."

See relevant scripture below.

Luke 10:19 (NASB)

[19] Behold, I have given you authority to tread on serpents and scorpions, and over all the power of the enemy, and nothing will injure you.

Of course He was talking about His Authority (ours also in Jesus Name) over demons, darkness, and disease. In fact authority over all evil. This covered addiction and withdrawals too. The words hit my Spirit like an explosion of life with aggressive, yet loving authority.

[eph 6:12] For our struggle is not against [e]flesh and blood, but against the rulers, against the powers, against the world forces of this darkness, against the spiritual *forces* of wickedness in the heavenly *places*. NASB

A Fight to the Finish (Message version)

[EPHESIANS6:10-12] And that about wraps it up. God is strong, and he wants you strong. So take everything the Master has set out for you, well-made weapons of the best materials. And put them to use so you will be able to stand up to everything the Devil throws your way. This is no afternoon athletic contest that we'll walk away from and forget about in a couple of hours. This is for keeps, a life-or-death fight to the finish against the Devil and all his angels.

Instantly, my eyes were opened to see the demonic culprits in the unseen world. I hit them 3 ways: HARD, FAST, AND CONTINUOUSLY with the NAME OF JESUS. The Bible says that demons must bow to the Name of Jesus. It was totally amazing; I felt like a man from another world. I felt like Samson slaying the Philistines with the jawbone of the ass. This awesome energy and unstoppable drive was just coursing through me. Every time I would speak the Name of Jesus, His Holy and Massive Supernatural Power, would wreak havoc against the powers of darkness. I could literally see the evil spirits back off, each time I would enforce the Victory of Calvary, through the Name of Jesus. I could see them backing off about six inches, every time I spoke against them with Jesus name. They looked like a thick and ugly cloud filled with grotesque, gargoyle like faces. It was very satisfying giving them what they deserve. They are the objects of Gods Holy wrath and God is pleased for them to flee when we speak Jesus Name. It was not just a spiritual thing but also a physical and mental sense of authority over the demons.

Each time I would speak the Name, my body would be employed literally throwing punches and my mind was like a steel trap in incisive declaration. Scripture backs up this physical and mental experience in Spiritual authority.

(PHYSICAL AND MENTAL STRENGTH AND ABILITY) OVER ALL

THE POWER THAT THE ENEMY (POSSESSES), AND NOTHING

SHALL IN ANY WAY HARM YOU". Luke 10:19b Amplified Bible

¹² And from the days of John the Baptist until

the present time, the kingdom of heaven has endured violent assault, and violent men seize it by force [as a precious prize—a share in the heavenly kingdom is sought with most ardent zeal and intense exertion]. Matt 11:12 (AMP)

Chapter 7

DEMONS FLEE

I continued to pound the demon forces into submission, through the Name of Jesus Christ, which is one of the ultimate offensive weapons we have at our disposal. It is the Spiritual equivalent of nukes. My two friends who were with me, thought I was having an emotional breakdown, seeing how I was punching and spiritually driving out unseen forces. I remember them grabbing my arms, pleading with me to settle down. I continued undeterred, I was fed up with the rotten devils and now I had their number and was really enforcing Victory in Jesus Name. As the last vestige of the demonic horde and cloud disappeared out the door, another cloud appeared in the room. Actually it was more like a mist or lovely fog, as soon as it manifested there was a wonderful Light, Beauty and Glory manifested. It was the Shekinah Glory Cloud of the Lord.

2 Chronicles 5:14 NASB so that the priests could not stand to minister because of the cloud, for the glory of the Lord filled the house of God.

Truly, the same Glory of the same God of Israel, filled that little banana shack that momentous night, in the hills of the North Coast of New South Wales. Instantly the withdrawal symptoms vanished and I knew I was delivered from all drugs. I was now filled with great joy and the presence of God flooded through me, like an ocean wave. My two friends who had watched all this take place, were now weeping in repentance for their sins. It was a remarkable miracle, of not only deliverance for me, but also of a deep and powerful conversion/salvation for my great friends. We all knelt together in the Presence of the Lord. My friends Wayne and Blanche gave their hearts to Jesus and I consecrated mine. There was such a precious and beautiful anointing of the Holy Spirit; it was so awesome after all the demonic oppression and darkness. We were now in Gods glorious presence. We all agreed that drugs and alcohol must be eradicated from our lives forever and we knew the power of God was present to back up our agreement. In fact, shortly after, to demonstrate our commitment we went and pulled up some huge marijuana plants that were growing nearby the shack and threw them into the flooded creek. It was so much fun we had an hilarious time doing it.

¹⁹ "Again I say to you, that if two of you agree on earth about anything that they may ask, it shall be done for them [a]by My Father who is in heaven" Matthew 18:19 (NASB)

I'm sure you will agree that this was a great victory over darkness, it was glorious. "THE WONDERS OF HIS LOVE AND THE TRIUMPHS OF HIS GRACE" The line of a grand hymn by Charles Wesley sums up the experience perfectly. I truly understand how Charles Wesley felt when he also penned the classic that exclaimed "O FOR A THOUSAND TONGUES TO SING MY GREAT REDEEMERS PRAISE." If I had a thousand tongues, indeed I would never have been able to express my appreciation and elation at Jesus wonderful transforming intervention, in my ravaged life. The modern colloquialism"WOW"in my estimation stands for" Wonder of Wonders." WOW Jesus! Say it backwards, WOW Lord! WOW, GLORY, HALLELUJAH, PRAISE THE LORD! GLORY, GLORY, GLORY! One could go on ad infinitum, in endless expressions of praise. That night marked a major turning point, now I was not just a carnal believer; I was now a disciple of Jesus. I'm talking about being under the authority of His Word, His Spirit, His Love, in fact being His total servant and of course His child.

[31] So Jesus was saying to those Jews who had believed Him, "If you continue in My word, *then* you are truly disciples of Mine; John 8:31 (NASB)

FREE AT LAST, FREE AT LAST, THANK GOD ALMIGHTY, I'M FREE AT LAST! (Dr Martin Luther King Jr)

"OLD THINGS HAD PASSED AWAY, ALL THINGS ARE BECOME NEW". II Corinthians 5; 17. KJV

I was now free from the filthy chains of addiction, which had almost choked the life out of me. I was truly "A NEW CREATURE" I was now unmistakably, irrevocably, one who was" IN CHRIST",

When I awoke the next morning, it was truly beautiful; the Australian bush was radiating all its glory with unique flora and fauna. I stood at the door of the shack and for some reason; I had a strong desire to look through an old rubbish box, which I had noticed under the shack. As I looked, I saw an old Bible, just what Dr Jesus ordered! I started to feed on the Scriptures. A couple of hours later, Wayne, Blanche and I decided to take a walk down the creek to the next farmhouse which was the home of Craig, a local cosmic philosopher and man about town. I had met him only once before. At the time, he seemed to be in the midst of some kind of a deal and he was not sociable at all. Now, as we walked to his house, we noticed these girls singing and dancing in his yard. We asked what they were doing; they said Craig had given his heart to Jesus and that he had just been baptized in the creek that was running through his farm. They said that all of Heaven was rejoicing over Craig's salvation and that they were walking and leaping and praising God for joy. I remember being deeply impressed, by the light in their eyes and the absolute shining joy upon their faces. One girl in particular was a great witness to my life. She was a real stunner, spiritually, as well as other more natural ways too. She was a missionary to the hippies, as I would later discover, she had been saved after 2 years studying Buddhism in India and Indonesia. She would later become my wife, Diana. (What an encounter of vast significance) Her story is huge also.

This was a miracle, not only were we zapped by the Holy Ghost, at our place in the banana shack, but half a mile down river Craig and a bunch of his friends had been radically converted from drugs and occultism, just recently also. It seemed there was a revival in the whole valley and area, which later we were to discover was a mind blowing reality. This was a classic revival that swept the entire region.

Chapter 8

REVIVAL/ SUNFLOWER RESTAURANT

There was a whole bunch of people I met that day, who were to become good friends in Christ, right up till the present day. One was to become my wife. I also lived in Craig's house with him, prior to both of us getting married. We had some astounding times of fellowship and spiritual discovery, as we grew together in Jesus Christ. There was a real revival in progress amongst the hippy/alternative lifestyle people in Mullumbimby/ Byron Bay. There was a vegetarian restaurant called "The Sunflower" in downtown Mullumbimby in 1977 which was being run by a hippy/ musician who had become known as "Mushroom Michael", because of his prolific consumption of hallucinogenic. (Psilocybin) mushrooms.

Well, Michael who was Jewish by birth, also claimed to be a Buddhist. But one night he was in the rainforest hills "tripping out on Mushrooms" and he actually fell off a cliff. The amazing thing was that he had been hiking in the rainforest at night on hallucinogens, he said he believed the "Universe" would safely guide him. (I did this myself once in Nimbin and didn't realize I was bleeding and covered in a multitude of blood sucking leeches until the light of dawn revealed it) Anyway, while Mike was in transit from the clifftop to the rocks below, he found himself calling out to Jesus to save him, and, Glory to God, he only incurred minor injuries. He instantly embraced Jesus as his Messiah and Lord and carried his Amplified Bible at all times now in his shoulder bag. He read it aloud all day long to anyone who would listen to him too!

The only problem was that even though he had become a follower of Christ, local gossips claimed he had not stopped consuming the psilocybin "Gold Top" mushrooms. As a matter of fact, I believe he did stop the mushrooms, but he sometimes displayed quite eccentric behavioral patterns, which may have led people to believe he still ate them. Mike was a bona fide artist and musician and as such he had the rightful claim to be eccentric, as many artists are. Also, the Joy of the Lord can sometimes make people wonder what drug a Spirit Filled Christian is on. (I always say God has His own brand of LSD—LOVE, SALVATION AND DELIVERANCE. He has the best Speed too—GODSPEED . Remember too that JESUS IS THE REAL THING—not Coke. The Holy Spirit gives Power to the saints who go marching into His Presence!

I remember my older brother Denis thinking I was on some kind of new drug, when I first stayed at his house as a Christian. He said my face was shining and looked like I had applied some kind of glistening oil to it. I remember I used to pray all day in my bedroom at his house and also read my Bible. Oftentimes, I would feel these amazing warm raindrops that felt so exhilarating falling on me, and I felt great surges of Gods Love, Grace and Power washing through my being, every time a drop fell on my head. This was a miracle, as I was indoors and it wasn't even raining outside. As I look back, I realize it was what the Bible terms "The Latter Rain" This is a term used to describe the latter day outpouring of the Holy Spirit, on all flesh. (It is interesting that in the Old Testament, they anointed with physical oil and poured a "horn" of oil on the anointees head. It is said a "horn" contained up to a quart of oil.) The anointing of the Spirit in the New Testament is with the Spiritual "Oil of Gladness" or Joy.

1. Proverbs 16:15

In the light of the king's countenance is life; and his favour is as a cloud of the latter rain. KJV

(Remember also how the people thought the disciples were drunk on the day of Pentecost when they were filled with the Holy Spirit.) See below.

ACTS 2:12-17 NASB And they all continued in amazement and great perplexity, saying to one another, "What does this mean?" [13] But others were mocking and saying, "They are full of [n] sweet wine."

Peter's Sermon

[14] But Peter, [o]taking his stand with the eleven, raised his voice and declared to them: "Men of Judea and all you who live in Jerusalem, let this be known to you and give heed to my words. [15] For these men are not drunk, as you suppose, for it is *only* the [p]third hour of the day; [16] but this is what was spoken of through the prophet Joel:

[17] 'AND IT SHALL BE IN THE LAST DAYS,' God says, 'THAT I WILL POUR FORTH OF MY SPIRIT ON ALL [q]MANKIND;

Mike was a very beautiful and compassionate person and he had a heart of gold. I remember him telling me he had recently received an inheritance from his grandfather of $40,000. He said he had read in the Bible to give to whoever asks of you. So he walked up the main street with the cash in a bag slung over his shoulder, he said he gave the lot away to whoever asked for it for whatever purpose. This of course, was taking the scriptural injunction out of context. Though, it did show Mikes willingness to obey Jesus instructions. He had a lovely heart, even if in his newly converted zeal, he may have acted unwisely.

The sad part is when I last saw him in the early 1990s, he was suffering some tough health problems. The awesome thing was that God really used Mike and his little "SUNFLOWER RESTAURANT," as a marshalling center in the region, in bringing people to Christ.

Michael was also giving free meals, to whoever came into his restaurant. Some mature Christians, started to frequent the place and to help cook and serve food. One was my future wife, Diana Neave, who had only recently completed a Vision Bible College Diploma in Sydney. Prior to her salvation in 1974 she had spent two years in India studying Buddhism and meditating, seeking truth. She realized that some Christians she met in India were the only ones who showed her true love. This had led to her coming to faith in Jesus as Lord. She had sensed a strong leading to come to Mullumbimby to do missionary work amongst the alternative hippy scene. She was working in association with Bruce Bridgeland; a Spirit filled lay Baptist minister, who along with his wife Norma had a strong love for the hippy kids. They gave of their time, money and whole lives to touch the "freaks." Bruce was a man with a great knowledge of the Bible and he would come around to teach the Word of God and reach out to the new babes in Christ, that were being birthed in the Sunflower Restaurant. It seemed new people wandered in and were being saved everyday there, and at this stage there was no pastor or leadership or church structure whatever. Most of the people were being zapped sovereignly by God. Some with no actual human contact at all. It was a true revival that was totally mind-blowing.

At one point there about 17 young men and women new hippy converts sleeping on the floor of the restaurant. They had no where else to go. Mike let anyone stay regardless of no room available. It was amazing there was no improper conduct between the boys and girls either, even though we slept squashed together as there was little room on the floor. Obviously this was not a perfect situation for spiritual growth but Gods Grace was huge in that wild and wooly but truly genuine Holy Revival.

God knew that many who were wandering in the occult world of counterfeit spiritual activity were in fact hungering and thirsting after the truth. In light of this, God visited the North Coast hills and Byron Bay with a genuine, made in Heaven, Holy Ghost revival. There was no advertising, not even any organized churches involved at the initial stages. God just blitzed the region. The miracle is that many people, who were converted in this move of God, are now fulltime ministers, or powerful leadership Christians in strong Biblical churches. Of course this move of God developed and progressed into birthing a number of churches and a powerful Christian Community that is not recounted in this volume.

It is very interesting that Corrie Ten Boom, the Christian leader and author of "The Hiding Place" fame, had visited the area in the 1950s and had prophesied of a coming revival. She foresaw the occultism that was yet to build in intensity in the region and said the Spirit of the Lord would raise a standard, in the next generation which would result in much salvation and deliverance.

Chapter 9

GODS PRESCRIPTION

God's wisdom is far greater than our own and He knows exactly what we need, to bring us into the fullness of our inheritance in Jesus Christ. I count it a glorious honor and privilege, to have been a part of this magnificent and heavenly visitation amongst the wild and wonderful hippy/surfers on the North Coast of NSW. Not just because it was exciting, totally spontaneous and easily some of the most wonderful times of my life. But also it proved to me Gods love and concern for the individual, namely me. (And my friends) I don't believe I would have made it into Christian fellowship, if I had been in a status quo, standard church situation, be it charismatic, evangelical or whatever. This way I could see God in action and know that He was a very real Being and that Christianity was not just an earthly organization of rules. This was sometimes like being back in the Book of Acts, with the Early Church.

The late 1970s Revival, amongst the alternative subcultures in Northern NSW, was as yet unencumbered by doctrinal or cultural preferences, these patterns inevitably creep into any church, once "Divine Order" and church government is established. This is not to say, by any means, that I do not believe in church government and Divine order, I do, it is essential and Scriptural. What I am saying, is this, I was not ready at that time to flow into that kind of situation and God in His mercy and custom made care and deliverance, dropped me into a situation that would revive me. He saved my very earthly life, as well as my soul by placing me into this wonderful group of people having revival in Jesus. Day by day, line upon line, precept upon precept, here a little and there a little, from one degree of glory to another. Structure did start to come, mainly in the form of Bruce Bridgeland leading the Bible studies in his home. He taught good solid principles from the Word and we also had powerful times of prayer, praise and worship.

A local Pentecostal lay preacher called Terry also started coming and providing valuable input in the area of evangelism and spiritual gifts, both Terry and Bruce did a wonderful and sacrificial job in the early days, in providing sound and balanced teaching as well as living lives that were a wholesome and realistic Christian example to the kids. Both Terry and Bruce had ceased to have any input or responsibility, by the time a church was formerly established under different leadership. Bruce has now gone to be with Jesus and great will be his reward in Heaven for the years of wonderful missionary work, he did amongst the lost and broken kids on the North Coast of New South Wales. Full credit must also go to his wife Norma who put up with a houseful of hippies, many nights until the early morning hours. Not to mention her releasing Bruce for the amazing time he put into his ministry. They managed to do all of this, as well as own and manage a large business. There are many others that could be mentioned; who were used of God in this move of The Spirit but this book is not intended to elaborate on the formation, of what was to become a fully structured church. Sadly, what began as a mighty move of the Holy Spirit eventually later became extreme in areas of personal shepherding teaching and consequently ran into some major problems. Thank God though that many who were fruits of the original revival, have gone on into other areas of growth and responsibility in the Body of Christ.

In August 1977, I moved from the N.S.W. North Coast to the Eastern Suburbs of Sydney, which were my old stomping grounds. It was also the very place where God had what became known as Hillsong City congregation to hold its inaugural services, as it turned out; I was in their first church meetings within a few weeks of the start. There were about 30 in attendance in those days. Now it is one of Australia's and the world's major churches. It is influential worldwide and quite a few of the key early members in Hillsong had come from ministry links to the great revival that blazed through Byron Shire NSW circa 1977-82. What was then known as the Coogee fellowship which was linked with the North Coast revival also brought key people to Hillsong, particularly in the music ministry.

White Hot Glory from Heaven!

I remember one of the early house church meetings I was in at Rose Bay, Sydney. During the worship time, I was hit with one of the most awesome anointings I have ever experienced in my life. My arms went straight up. They felt like they were rockets on the way to the moon. I remember that I could not bring them down and my hands felt like "WHITE HOT ELECTRICITY". My hands were burning with this awesome and intense heat that literally seared into my palms. While this was in progress, I had a distinct impression that no sickness or disease could stand in the presence of that anointing. The ecstasy of this experience was indeed too much to handle. I realized that my ecstatic shouts and utterances were disrupting the meeting. So I asked to be excused and went to an ocean cliff top to worship God and cool out. I have never experienced that measure of unction in that way again but I knew that I must lay hands upon the sick at every opportunity in future. A lady who was present at the meeting that night said she saw beautiful golden colored angels in the room when that anointing was in manifestation.

I enjoyed being back in the city, especially the church and all, but I was now in a far more intense spiritual warfare because of being right in the midst of the old drug scene, so to speak. I made a point of reaching out to my friends in the drug scene. It was a much harder job to reach them with the Gospel than I had previously anticipated.

Chapter 10

TWO FRIENDS AND CASUALTIES

There were two in particular that I put an extraordinary amount of prayer and time into, their names were Chris and Peter. Chris had been tied up in heavy amphetamine abuse from the age of around 15. He had come into contact with a drug chemist who had manufactured the stuff. This pusher then gave Chris quantities to sell on credit. Chris never made any money but became his own best customer, consuming vast quantities of the villainous substance. It was a tragic waste of a young life. Chris was brilliant young guy with a great sense of humour. He could converse with great knowledge on any given subject. What made it even more of a crying shame was the fact that Chris was extremely intelligent and was an amazingly talented musician. His lightning fast and intricate lead guitar riffs bordered on virtuosity. If he had developed and honed his skills, who knows what he may have achieved. His brother became a notable jazz guitarist.

Chris started consuming tranquilizers and narcotics, to bring him down off the "speed" binges. Soon he was a hopeless addict and would stumble about in an absolute stupor most of his waking hours. Chris would take a whole bottle of 50 Valium tablets and it would hardly slow him down. Often with huge doses in his system, he would still be conscious and falling about like a hopeless drunk. I have never seen anyone consume such prodigious quantities of mind altering chemicals. I remember him falling from the third story of a Bondi beach hotel onto the pavement, he

41

then got up and walked away with his head bleeding, not realizing it had even happened. Another time he fell from the top of a steep flight of steps, head over heels. He got up at the bottom and stumbled off, unaware it even occurred. Once I sat on him all night at a party so he would not wander outside into the traffic. God directed me to spend much time, after my own conversion, with Chris.

I would witness to him and pray for him repeatedly, when he was coherent. He came to church and gave his life to Jesus and gained the victory for a period of time over drugs but then he slid back into his chemical self destruction. He freely acknowledged that Jesus was the way but did not taste of the resurrection victory in his own life. Chris slid deeper and deeper into oblivion. The amazing thing was that he lived quite a few more years, before he overdosed and died.

Peter, another friend was also terribly overtaken by drug abuse which finally claimed him in 1985. Peter had a devastating motorcycle accident in 1970 which almost cost him his foot. The surgeons saved it but he never regained its full mobility. I met Peter in 1971 through his brother Des. I had gone to school with Des; he also was a great friend. Prior to the accident, Peter was an Australian champion spear fisherman and abalone diver. In the hospital, he had received a lot of morphine for pain control, maybe this is how he had developed an interest in drug experimentation which seemed out of character, since Peter had never even smoked or drank in his entire life up until age 25.

He had received a damages payout, for his motorcycle accident. This occurred at a time when he was also being seduced into the world of dope smoking, he had came into contact with some traffickers (in hashish), and was persuaded to buy a pound of it. One thing led to another and before long he was a well known dealer on Sydney's Eastern Suburb beaches. This situation went on for years and eventually he reluctantly received heroin as payment for a hashish deal. (The men told him they would either rip him off or give him the hard drug as payment.) Well, as you can no doubt guess, Peter became severely addicted to hard drugs. I had a real love for Peter and indeed his entire family.

After my Christian conversion, I would frequently be praying for his salvation and going around telling him about Jesus. Well, Peter came to church with me one Sunday night. During the meeting the pastor had a word of knowledge, (a Divine knowing about someone's life from God) that someone in the service had injured their foot in a motorcycle accident and they were in constant pain from it. This blew Peter away as it described his situation perfectly, even more amazing, during the service he was sitting behind a concrete pillar that hid him totally from the pastors view, as he did not want to be singled out (to be Bible bashed), he said.

Well God certainly had his number, as the pastor did not know Peter and had never heard of him. He could not even see him in the service. Peter went forward and received Jesus as his Savior. He was instantly set free from pain in his foot and as a bonus, was set free from the power of heroin. It was a real miracle, for 6 weeks, Peter lived totally drug free and came to visit me every day to pray and counsel with me. One day, six weeks later, Peter came to see me with tears in his eyes and told me how he had fallen (from grace) back into drugs, (he also lost his healing in his foot). He was deeply grieved and we asked the Lords forgiveness for him together in prayer.

The Good News is that Peter did manage to stay off heroin. But sadly, he felt that he needed to be on a methadone maintenance program. (Which I believe he could have avoided had he trusted God more.) The dosage of methadone Peter was on did not cause intoxication, it was just enough to bring equilibrium and freedom from discomfort. He was having trouble sleeping so he received some prescription medication to help him sleep. The only trouble was, mixed with the methadone it contraindicated and was a lethal combination that caused a respiratory system collapse. Consequently, Peter died in his sleep in 1985 at the age of 39. To many this may sound like a total defeat, but Peter's life was different after his experience with Christ.

He was freed from dependence on illegal narcotics even though he was not totally delivered from prescription drugs. Had he been willing to walk in a deeper degree of discipleship with Jesus, he could have entered into total freedom. The Good News is I believe we will see him in Heaven, I believe Chris made it too.

I have shared about Peter and Chris, to give an idea of the ministry that God had me involved in during the early 80's. People with severe drug and alcohol problems, usually need extremely intensive care and support, if they are going to make it into true freedom in Jesus Christ. I found that it was one thing to lead a person with drug problems to Christ but an entirely more difficult battle, to bring them into a new life with victory over drugs or alcohol. I believe that they need to be removed from the whole environment of drugs, old associates, etc., for a period of at least 12 months. During this time there needs to be daily Christian fellowship, prayer, worship and teaching, to bring the deliverance that is needed. I thank God that I had this and that is why I'm alive to tell my story. That is why God has enabled me to help found and pastor a church in Australia. I have also had the privilege of being senior pastor of two great churches in California. I have had the opportunity to preach the Gospel in evangelism all around the world since believing in Christ as well.

There are many other lives I could write about, many with totally victorious and glorious endings. But for some reason I tell the story of Chris and Peter to highlight the need for specialized ministries to reach these types of people. God has been so good to me over the years. His goodness and compassion are beyond our ability to comprehend. Psalm 136 says over and over again that:

"HIS MERCY ENDURETH FOREVER" KJV

I know it is the Power and Grace of God that has sustained and kept me. He has opened doors that no man can open. I have, by the Grace of God, preached in Australia, Mexico, Indonesia, England, France, Nigeria, as well as in many parts of the U.S.A. (other places as well).

Paul Sames preaching in Bali, Indonesia, 2004

Paul Sames and wife Diana Sames enjoying dinner, 2005

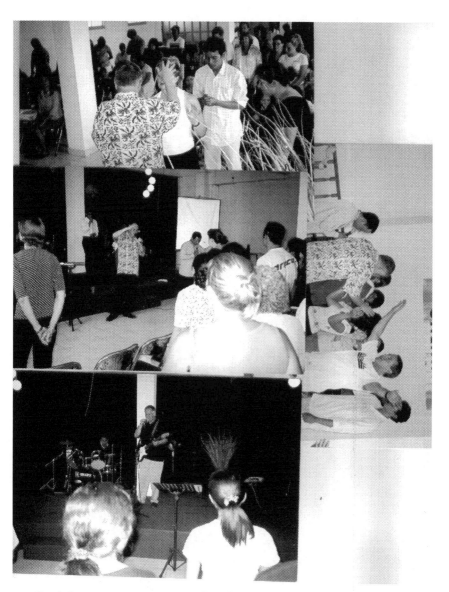

Paul Sames ministry in Word and Music in Indonesian churches

Paul Sames playing guitar circa early 70s, also
friends and family collage from 70s and 80s

Paul and wife Diana somewhere in Caribbean 2007

Paul Sames with 2 ministers and inmates ministering in Juarez federal prison Mexico. 3 men on right are doing life and serving Jesus. Powerful time in God! Great missionary friend Dan Hoyl was sadly not in this photo but was there with me. Godspeed Dan! See you in Heaven!

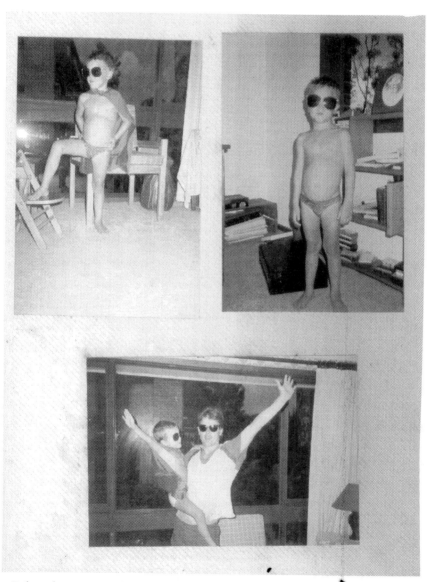

Beloved son Aaron Sames (1981-2010) pictured in 1985 at 4 years old.

Awesome son Aaron Sames (1981-2010) with Dad
Paul at 14 years of age in 1995 in California.

Mighty Man Aaron Sames! A man with a Heart of Fire and Love for God and people. Pictured in his early 20s in Florida. Beloved and much missed by all who knew him. He had friends aged from 8---80. Aaron valiantly battled cancer for 4 years. See you in Heaven Aaro!

Paul Sames ministering on altar call in Jakarta, Indonesia.

Leading Buddhist Patriarch in Java in prayer
to Jesus for Salvation and Healing

Paul Sames leading worship with beloved son and guitarist/
songwriter Reuben Sames at Aaron Sames memorial service 2010.
Aaron is playing basketball at 12 years old in pic on screen in photo.

SHADOW TO SUBSTANCE

Part 2 (written on average 7 years later)

Chapter 11

Religiosity revealed

I have often felt that pseudo religiosity, is the greatest enemy of the true and living God. Jesus took a harder line with the Pharisees of His day, than any of the so called gross sinners such as adulterers, publicans and prostitutes. (see verse).

Matthew 23:13-15 (NASB)

Eight Woes

[13] "But woe to you, scribes and Pharisees, hypocrites, because you shut off the kingdom of heaven [a]from [b]people; for you do not enter in yourselves, nor do you allow those who are entering to go in. [14] [[c]Woe to you, scribes and Pharisees, hypocrites, because you devour

widows' houses, and for a pretense you make long prayers; therefore you will receive greater condemnation.]

¹⁵ "Woe to you, scribes and Pharisees, hypocrites, because you travel around on sea and land to make one [d]proselyte; and when he becomes one, you make him twice as much a son of [e]hell as yourselves.

Sadly, even Christianity, which is Gods ultimate covenant with man, has become ensnared with the spirit of religion and in many cases has become a mere parody or shadow, of its true substance. This is nothing short of tragic because true New Covenant Christianity is the highest, most joyous and fulfilling life available to any man or woman on earth.

"And Jesus said unto them, I am the bread of life: he that cometh to me shall never hunger; and he that believeth on me shall never thirst." John 6:35. King James Version KJV

As a boy I was raised in a highly structured denominational situation. This was well before the charismatic renewal had come on the scene. At around age 12, I rebelled and was led astray by the glamour of sin. I reasoned that I was bored by the repetition, rote and ritual of church. I had just started being attracted to girls and I wrongly imagined so called "cool" girls would not like me if I was going to church. (I also was being influenced by the lyrics of The Beatles and similar bands and the allure of

60s psychedelia, that was constantly in the news at that time.) I abandoned the church at an early age and got involved in a full blown search for deeper meaning, purpose and inner fulfillment. This led me on a deep quest into different spiritual teachings and philosophies ranging from astrology, to Tibetan Buddhism and astral traveling, to UFOlogy. I also became involved with drug experimentation and was a great psychedelic disciple, being fascinated by the teachings of men like Dr Timothy Leary and Ram Dass. (Dr Richard Alpert). At that time I was open to every so called "ism" and "ology" imaginable, as I was desperately hungry to get the very heart of reality, as I liked to term it.

2 Tim 4:3 For the time will come when they will not endure sound doctrine; but after their own lusts shall they heap to themselves teachers, having itching ears;

4 And they shall turn away their ears from the truth, and shall be turned unto fables. King James Version (KJV)

In January 1974, after a number of years of "searching", I had a major "head on" encounter with Our Lord Jesus Christ that flooded me with seemingly endless and indescribable waves of cleansing Spiritual Fire and Compassion. The only way I can attempt to describe this experience, was that it felt like wave after wave of liquid love that just penetrated, permeated and saturated every fiber of my being. All of this happened after I called on the Name of Jesus. Prior to this awesome baptism in Fire, God had opened my eyes to the spiritual realm of darkness and showed me the minions of wickedness, it was terrifying but as soon as I cried "Jesus," the darkness fled and instead of sorrow there was joy and glory.

Eph 6:12 For we wrestle not against flesh and blood, but against principalities, against powers, against the rulers of the darkness of this world, against spiritual wickedness in high places.

Rom 10:13 For whosoever shall call upon the name of the Lord shall be saved. King James Version KJV

Since becoming a Christian and believer of the Gospel, one of the most discouraging aspects of my Christian experience, has been the shallow emptiness of some of the contemporary religious culture.

Firstly, let me say that I am a great believer in the local and Universal Church or Body of Christ, God does not call us to isolation but to be members in particular of His Family or church on Earth. I am writing this, not to discredit or demean the church (i.e. The Body of Christ) which is also described in Scripture as the Bride of Christ; I love the people of God, the Church militant and the Church triumphant.

I feel I need to address areas that could be a stumbling block to many potential new believers in Christ, especially as they seek to enter fellowship in a new church situation. Sadly, some church leaders have not been great examples of Christ likeness or Godliness; of course this should not be a surprise, as God is using weak imperfect vessels like us, to communicate His Eternal message of Love and Salvation.

I am convinced that the average Christian has not experienced the true joys and fulfillment, of genuine New Testament Christian fellowship. Much of modern Western style religious culture is completely centered on the cheerleading type of "Service". Now, while we in no wise wish to downplay the importance of preaching, teaching and worship, it is not just the "structured service," that is our service to God. I suspect that a lot of the problem lies in the cultural phenomenon of living an "image" in public or on television but once we get out of the service; there is an astounding lack of relationship with each other in a real sense.

I was once interviewed on a Christian television program. Prior to the cameras rolling, I was treated with indifference by the TV host and crew almost to the point of them being unaware I was present. The minute the "ACTION ON CAMERA" Cue was given, the host exploded into the persona of a warm and vibrant family member, who was so excited I was there to have fellowship with him. The minute the cameras stopped rolling, I was again almost ignored. When I attempted warm off camera fellowship, I was met with a professional "SINCERE" smile, which a used car salesman could have easily outdone. This was a great lesson for me, in the way some of the religious cultures operate.

The Greek word for true New Testament fellowship is "Koinonia" "or caring enough to share". Without Koinonia, Christianity is like an egg with a hollow shell, or black clouds with no rain. The very heart of God is relationship and He desires that we not only relate to Him, but to each other in a real and genuine way.

Ephesians 4:1 (NASB)

15 but [i]speaking the truth in love, [j]we are to grow up in all *aspects* into Him who is the head, *even* Christ, 16 from whom the whole body, being fitted and held together [k]by what every joint supplies, according to the [l]proper working of each individual part, causes the growth of the body for the building up of itself in love

Chapter 12

TV SITCOM OR REALITY?

We desperately need to erase the television image of relationship and develop real love and interaction. I have noticed that as a substitute for the dysfunctional nightmare that is often the real state of the western family situation, there is often this tendency to live out our lives via television and imprint the sitcom reality into our experience. (as a substitute for real life.) This allows millions to live out a television fantasy, thinking that life is one big saccharin sweet TV sitcom.

Unfortunately a "Christianized" version of this has flooded the church also. Large sections of the first world western church, are relationally bankrupt, by this I mean that there is very little real fellowship and Holy Spirit relationship apart from a few, "How ya doins" and "God bless yas" in the foyer, as we scurry out the door after service. Many churches seek to appease this relational vacuum, by this great cheer leading, high fiving, back slapping, hail fellow well met syndrome. For those who have ever tasted the awesome, heartfelt satisfaction of real Christian fellowship, this is a tragic heartbreaking excuse for real church life. No amount of ludicrous parading of fashion statements and expensive watches, $300 shoes and "strut your stuff" routines will even remotely compensate for genuine intimacy with God and each other.

I for one have had a gutful of religious cultural posturing, jockeying and parading. Sadly, oftentimes the worst and most intense versions of this take place among some ministers who seem to be under a desperate compulsion, to impress one another with some kind of prosperterian success routine. Some pastors conventions are characterized by the "big shots" (those with a thousand or more members) congregating in exclusive and elitist huddles. (In fact, some of the mega clerics may not even come into the conventions now at all but will stay in the "green room" with the other all star clergy and will only appear like a rock star, to perform) Sometimes any attempt by a "little shot" (i.e. pastor of small church or unknown evangelist) to be accepted is met, at best, with patronizing tones (or more usually) with disrespect and demeaning humor. I know this may sound harsh to some of you but this is not an exaggeration. Of course this does not mean that there are not many genuine, caring pastors of large churches. There are many wonderful leaders of mega churches. I love Arthur Blessit, one of the greatest evangelists in church history, in my opinion, who when told he could avoid the sheep by slipping out a side door at the church, said "No I want to be with the people, the more the better, God has called me to be with His people everywhere"—That's the right Spirit. It must be the Holy Spirit!

Listen to what St Paul said about some of the preachers of his era.

2 CORINTHIANS 11:4-24 JB Phillips version

Yet I cannot believe I am in the least inferior to these extra-special messengers of yours. Perhaps I am not a polished speaker, but I do know what I am talking about, and both what I am and what I say is pretty familiar to you.

7-10 Perhaps I made a mistake in cheapening myself (though I did it to help you) by preaching the Gospel without a fee? As a matter of fact I was only able to do this by "robbing" other churches, for it was what they paid me that made it possible to minister to you free of charge. Even when I was with you and very hard up, I did not bother any of you. It was the brothers who came from Macedonia who brought me all that I needed. Yes, I kept myself from being a burden to you then, and so I intend to do in the future. By the truth of Christ within me, no one shall stop my being proud of this independence through all Achaia!

¹¹⁻¹⁵ Does this mean that I do not love you? God knows it doesn't, but I am determined to maintain this boast, so as to cut the ground from under the feet of those who profess to be God's messengers on the same terms as I am. God's messengers? They are counterfeits of the real thing, dishonest practitioners, "God's messengers" only by their own appointment. Nor do their tactics surprise me when I consider how Satan himself masquerades as an angel of light. It is only to be expected that his agents shall have the appearance of ministers

of righteousness—but they will get their deserts one day.

If you like self-commendation, listen to mine!

[16] Once more, let me advise you not to look upon me as a fool. Yet if you do, then listen to what this "fool" has to boast about.

[17-21] I am not now speaking as the Lord commands me but as a fool who must be "in on" this business of boasting. Since all the others are so proud of themselves, let me do a little boasting as well. From your heights of superior wisdom I am sure you can smile tolerantly on a fool. Oh, you're tolerant all right! You don't mind, do you, if a man takes away your liberty, spends your money, makes a fool of you or even smacks your face? I am almost ashamed to say that I never did brave strong things like that to you. Yet in whatever particular they enjoy such confidence I (speaking as a fool, remember) have just as much confidence.

²² Are they Hebrews? So am I. Are they Israelites? So am I. Are they descendants of Abraham? So am I.

²³ Are they ministers of Christ? I have more claim to this title than they. This is a silly game but look at this list: I have worked harder than any of them. I have served more prison sentences! I have been beaten times without number. I have faced death again and again.

²⁴ I have been beaten the regulation thirty-nine stripes by the Jews five times.

²⁵ I have been beaten with rods three times. I have been stoned once. I have been shipwrecked three times. I have been twenty-four hours in the open sea.

²⁶⁻²⁷ In my travels I have been in constant danger from rivers and floods, from bandits, from my own countrymen, and from pagans. I have faced danger in city streets, danger in the

desert, danger on the high seas, danger among false Christians. I have known exhaustion, pain, long vigils, hunger and thirst, going without meals, cold and lack of clothing.

28-29 Apart from all external trials I have the daily burden of responsibility for all the churches. Do you think anyone is weak without my feeling his weakness? Does anyone have his faith upset without my longing to restore him?

30-31 Oh, if I am going to boast, let me boast of the things which have shown up my weakness! The God and Father of our Lord Jesus Christ, he who is blessed for ever, knows that I speak the simple truth.

Romans 12:16 (NASB)

16 Be of the same mind toward one another; do not be haughty in mind, but [a]associate with the lowly. Do not be wise in your own estimation.

Paul G. Sames

A pastor I knew from my early years (a genuine and successful pastor who has impacted the World for Christ) said that he attended a preacher's convention in a certain US city. He said he felt isolated and alienated, as he did not know any one there well and he noticed the big shots tended to be gathering in exclusive circles, hobnobbing with each other. At one point he told how a prominent pastor came over and asked "How many ya runnin?"(Meaning "How many congregants attending your church?") When the pastor told him only 1500 at that time, he said the preacher just grunted and walked off, as if to say "Come back when you have got 5000."

This experience was such a shock for the pastor, that he told his whole church that the so called "'big shot" preacher was not worth a tin of rotten fish in his estimation. I agree wholeheartedly. That kind of attitude is so far from Christ likeness, it would be laughable, if it were not such a travesty.

Romans 12:10 (NASB)

[10] *Be* devoted to one another in brotherly love; [a]give preference to one another in honor;

Pope Francis elected in March 2013 has addressed this issue in his actions and lifestyle as a cardinal and has gone out of his way as Pope to be a humble servant leader. He does foot washings of prisoners, catches buses, even asking for Catholic and non catholic Christians for prayer and input, it is a refreshing new breeze in the Body of Christ.

(For example, when he was introduced during a large Christian meeting in Buenos Aires where over 5,000 evangelical protestant leaders were in attendance, Pope Francis (then Cardinal Bergoglio) knelt down in front of the evangelical pastors and asked them to lay hands on him and bless him! Every year, as Cardinal, he would join his evangelical brothers (pastors) for their annual weeklong retreat—not as a guest speaker to teach, but as one of them.—kcm blog excerpt)

Chapter 13

FOOTBALL GAME OR FELLOWSHIP?

Just because a thousand people gather and shout, praise and even jump up and down in effusive displays of enthusiasm, with hearty backslapping, then turning to the neighbor on each side in the meeting and saying something on the preachers cue, this is no substitute for relational interaction and fellowship. Thank God for great exuberant anointed services, we absolutely need it, we need the outpouring of the Holy Spirit in our meetings but we must just as surely make time for unstructured anointed friendships, with each other (fellowship is just an old world term for friendship). This friendship time does not have to be "religious," in the sense of having to be doing Bible studies and praying or whatever. It is just quality time being friends and loving one another.

Hebrews 10:24-25

(NASB) ²⁴ and let us consider how to stimulate one another to love and good deeds, ²⁵ not forsaking our own assembling together, as is the habit of some, but encouraging *one another*; and all the more as you see the day drawing near.

Dr Yonggi Cho, pastor of the worlds largest church in Seoul, Korea (about 1 million strong at time of writing) says that one of the big problems in the US church is the lack of relationship after services. He said that in Korea if the service lasts 2 hrs, then the people will spend 2 hrs fellowshipping after the structured side of the service. He says that the time we spend with each other after the worship and Word, altar call etc, is just as much a part of the service. This is the time, when we through love "serve" one another and minister to each other, without even realizing it. Please understand I am not talking about getting together in huddles; holding hands and spiritualizing everything, no we are just talking about "hanging out" with each other developing "relationship" and if prayer spontaneously flows out of this, fine, but these are not times where there is legislated spiritual activity. Sometimes the most spiritual thing you can do is have a good laugh at dinner with friends.

Yonggi Cho said that in the US and west, Christians run for the parking lot to escape as soon as possible after the Amen. This is sad, because people miss out on developing friendships within the Body. When Eph 4:16 talks about the Body being joined together and compacted by that which every "joint" supplies it is talking about relationships. (The joints are relationships) In the arm, the elbow joint relates the forearm to the upper arm, in the leg, the knee joint relates the lower leg to the thigh and so on. Without relationship, the body parts would have no relevancy to each other or to themselves; in fact they would be reduced to anatomical trash. We can use this analogy, to become aware of the crucial importance of relationships within the Body of Christ.

No Individual Interpretation

As Christians who are born again and Spirit filled Bible believers, we know that the Bible is not for esoteric interpretation. We learn from church history that this was the heresy and mistake of the early church era Gnostics. The Gnostics considered that they had special knowledge and revelation that was not available to the average Christian; they specialized in esoteric interpretation of Scripture. In other words, they claimed to be able to see hidden messages in the Scripture. This opened the door for all sorts of "revelation" that seemed exceedingly spiritual but in reality opened the door for another spirit and another gospel. Eastern mysticism and New Age philosophy operate on this same premise, they even read the Bible and quote Scripture but do not stick to exoteric (i.e. literal, it means what it says, comparing scripture with scripture) interpretation which orthodox Christianity requires.

2 Peter 1:20 NASB

²⁰ knowing this first, that no prophecy of scripture is of private interpretation.

Rev 22:18 For I testify unto every man that heareth the words of the prophecy of this book, If any man shall add unto these things, God shall add unto him the plagues that are written in this book:

19 And if any man shall take away from the words of the book of this prophecy, God shall take away his part out of the book of life, and out of the holy city, and from the things which are written in this book. King James KJV

Having said that, I believe that modern Christianity has degenerated in many instances, to a shallow hull of the early New Testament experience. In some important areas, the New Age religions have often taken the initiative from the church. This is sad because the church of the living God is called to be the originator and definitive article as it were. As in every other area the Body of Christ is called to be the place where the most awesome, fulfilling, and wonderful relationship take place. After all, God is the original "family maker" and the family is where the most exciting, wonderful and precious relationships take place.

Psalm 68:6 God setteth the solitary in families: he bringeth out those which are bound with chains: but the rebellious dwell in a dry land. KJV

Chapter 15

LONELY IN THE CROWD?

The church is Gods family and we cannot have family relations if all we ever see is the back of someone's head and then offer a few religious platitudes on the way to the car. I believe this is a serious problem in the modern mega church. How do I know? I have firsthand experience of this, because some of the loneliest experiences I have ever had have been sitting in a large church meeting or convention. Even though the ministry is awesome and the praise is off the Richter scale, without true "joints" or "relationships" it is a hollow experience, somehow it can make one feel inferior. This is probably because it makes one feel alienated, as the powerful service seems disconnected from the individual in the pew and it makes one feel inferior to the high flyers on the stage. Often times the pastors/leaders and ministry team are having deep fellowship with each other but it doesn't reach down to the church member in the pew.

Let me qualify these statements by saying that it is often not the local pastor's fault; one of the big culprits in this syndrome is the very nature of western society today. It is a society of individuals where people live as kings unto themselves; community awareness is sacrificed on the altar of selfish individualism. The whole small town concept is often almost dead in today's first world culture. People no longer have any time or place to gather to form true relationships and because of time constraints church functions are made up for the most part, of organized worship where we have brief pleasantries and then spend time in corporate worship and listen to preaching and teaching. Meaningful friendships are hard to form in church. (Again, I am not saying the corporate side of worship is unimportant, it is vital and Scriptural).

Also when a family moves to a new city, finding a place of love and friendship is difficult. I believe God wants us to spend time in each others presence, not just a few minutes either, we need regularly scheduled time (both quality and quantity) in each others presence, if we are ever going to have the deep fellowship that Jesus intended for His people in the New Testament. I realize this seems a total impossibility, given the nature of today's world, and the frenzied schedules that most folks have to keep. Also, there are the sheer distances, that people attending the same church live from each other, in major metropolitan areas. It is not at all unusual for church members today to be separated by an hours drive at freeway speeds. In more olden times people would live within sound of the church bell and they would walk together to church, consequently, not only were people close to their place of worship, but they were close to those with whom they worshipped and everybody worked together, socialized together, fellowshipped and worshipped together. This was a major healing and integrating force within a community, this setup facilitated wholeness.

Modern medical studies by noted cardiologist and author Dr Dean Ornish, as well as many others, have found definite links between isolation and heart disease, as well as other serious diseases. People, who have a loving network of friends and family, are being found to have far less chance of succumbing to terminal illness and premature death. I believe Eph 4:16 speaks of the importance of not only holding fast to God but to each other in order that we may develop in relationship and love in Christ.

Ephesians 4:15-16 (NASB)

15 but [i]speaking the truth in love, [i]we are to grow up in all *aspects* into Him who is the head, *even* Christ,[16] from whom the whole body, being fitted and held together [a]by what

every joint supplies, according to the [b]proper working of each individual part, causes the growth of the body for the building up of itself in love.

Friends we need each other, whether we like it or not, we were not created to be self contained islands. Our interactive fellowship, ministers to each other, even if the basis of our mingling is not at all "spiritual" or "religious". God is a God of family and intimate and intricate relationship, He wants us to experience the amazing Love and Grace of Holy Spirit anointed families and friendships. Satan, on the other hand desires to alienate us and devalue our Christian and life experience. He wants us to feel like a faceless number or nobody; he knows that Gods great secret weapon against evil is loving relationships with Him and each other. The devil can't expertly counterfeit Gods LOVE. Gifts can be copied easily but Love is Gods Ultimate Reality and it is inimitable. Counterfeit love is easily detected by Gods Word and Treasury experts in much the same way that fake $100 bills are easily discerned by US Treasury agents. If you know the genuine in a deep way, it's easy to spot a fake.

Chapter 16

STAGE SET CHRISTIANITY?

When I speak of "pseudo religious culture," I speak of something which I believe is sometimes antichrist. The word Christ means "the anointed One and His Anointing". Pseudo religious culture is a facade, an "image management exercise in emptiness and veneer". It is like the old stage sets that were built in Hollywood, to make westerns. The facades of the storefronts looked like a real town with real buildings but it was only a storefront, an empty "image". You couldn't live there; it was not a real place. Pseudo religious culture, can harbor the worst kind of "keeping up with the spiritual Jones" (religious social climbing) It sometimes produces a competitive spiritual social climbing, amongst the congregation and leaders, which is frightening and discouraging to the genuine Christian, who is searching, hungering and thirsting after the "anointed Righteousness of true fellowship or Koinonia".

Pseudo religious culture is anti anointing and that is why I say it is antichrist. If one wants to be close to the "right" ministry, or part of the so perceived spiritual "elite," in a particular religious culture, then you had better be a "somebody" that will enhance the reputation of who you consort with. In addition, you had better have the right clothes, hairstyle and car etc, not to mention career.

My wife Diana and I visited a large church in another city. In fact, the pastor and the church had no idea we were pastors visiting from another town. The senior pastor instructed the junior associates to go to the area where the new folks in the service were asked to gather, so they could engage them in friendly conversation and fellowship after service and help them into church life. When we got to the gathering spot we immediately realized that the majority of young pastors were talking to each other, not the new people. A couple of pastors only, were engaged in a half hearted way with only a couple of people. We saw that the young pastors were far more interested in being in the presence of the famous senior minister, than to feed the sheep he had employed them to feed. I actually tried to engage one young minister in friendly dialogue and he was totally disinterested and kept looking over my shoulder for a glimpse of Rev Big. You might think I'm being unfair, or exaggerating, but this was a true case.

Thankfully, most churches aren't bound by this celebrity complex. Also in his defense, the famous pastor had a genuine desire to care for the people, which is why he employed the younger pastors, he was so busy with a huge ministry, and he couldn't help and talk to everyone in the church. The young pastors were overtaken by the desire to be the closest to the top pastor. (Wrong priorities). Consequently they were neglecting his sheep.

Spiritual Superfly?

When I first encountered the spirit motivating the true religionist, it was amazing to me how much it reminded me of the old "SUPERFLY" movie from the 70s. In the netherworld of drugs, the dealer is ignored, unless he is "holding" the "goods" and then he becomes the most popular person on the block. Everyone wants to be his friend and hopefully get some free "tastes" or doses of the drug. The minute the dealer is bereft of his product, then again he is a nobody, unless of course there is the promise of an imminent incoming shipment.

Dealers, who are drug and money rich, emanate an aura of mystique and speak in hushed secretive tones, to those they are doing business with. These people are held in great respect and are elevated to an idol like status in the drug culture. Some ministries when they arrive on "the religious scene" want to be lauded and spoken of as some kind of spiritual "Superfly." (a 1970s movie depicting a flamboyant drug dealer of the same name) They often have an entourage of associates, bodyguards and general hangers on (though I recognize for some genuine ministries, that security

& crowd control is needed) that evoke this mystique and image. These modern day Pharisees remain aloof and detached from fellowship with the people. They are rushed in the front pre service and rushed out the back post service, even when the crowds are small and they could easily mingle with the people.

One thing that tremendously impressed me about Billy Graham (a man who could easily justify remaining aloof, considering the magnitude of his ministry) when he was conducting a crusade in Sydney, Australia in 1979, was his genuine humility and love for the people. I happened to be standing a few feet from where his car had stopped to deliver him one evening. It was crusade starting time and this middle aged lady started talking to him, as he left his vehicle. The crowd of 50,000 plus were already singing the last hymns and his hosts were awaiting him on the platform. Dr Graham gave this lady, genuine time, love and attention; he treated her like she was the only one at the crusade. I remember thinking how gracious, Christ like and loving his attitude to her was. I have often wondered if this is the reason God has used Billy so vastly this past century. I suspect that his loving down to earth humility is probably why God has been able to use him so well. He always said he was just a farm boy and has no idea why God gave him such a high profile ministry.

Matt 23:11 But he that is greatest among you shall be your servant.

12 And whosoever shall exalt himself shall be abased; and he that shall humble himself shall be exalted.

13 But woe unto you, scribes and Pharisees, hypocrites! for ye shut up the kingdom of

heaven against men: for ye neither go in yourselves, neither suffer ye them that are entering to go in.

14 Woe unto you, scribes and Pharisees, hypocrites! for ye devour widows' houses, and for a pretence make long prayer: therefore ye shall receive the greater damnation. 15 Woe unto you, scribes and Pharisees, hypocrites! for ye compass sea and land to make one proselyte, and when he is made, ye make him twofold more the child of hell than yourselves. King James Version KJV

Chapter 16

GODS CORAL OR
PLASTIC MERMAIDS

Pseudo religious culture is an extreme rip off, because it has the audacity to claim that it is Gods Kingdom in operation. It is no more Gods Kingdom, than the old Disneyland submarine ride in Anaheim, California, is the Great Barrier Reef in Australia. I went on the old Disneyland sub once with my kids and it made me mad that people actually think all those plastic fish and mermaids are pretty. To me it was the height of a bad imitation and I thought it was sterile and sad that people loved it so much. It's not their fault though; most of them had never seen a genuine pristine coral reef. I have seen the real thing, I have snorkeled and scuba dived in the real Great Barrier Reef and Caribbean. I have seen the myriad corals and colors of Gods great masterpieces. As wonderful as the Disney imagineers may be, they can't hold a candle to Gods Omnicreative Masterpieces.

Note: At publishing time, the sub ride and plastic reef and indeed the whole of old Disneyland has long been demolished. Today we have a much better imitation marine experience at Discovery Cove in Orlando. It is much more natural and I have heard it is a beautiful experience. So hats off to the Disney Imagineers for following Gods blueprint for a natural experience.

The great tragedy in the Western church is that people are being sold a lie. People are sometimes partaking of a plastic religious counterfeit and are desperately trying to get excited about it, as being the genuine bona fide New Testament experience. The reason many swallow this lie, is the same reason that people and kids got excited, about the submarine ride on the plastic fake counterfeit reef. The only reason I can imagine people would make such a big deal about that ride is because they have never experienced the wonder, grandeur and timeless beauty of a God created coral reef. Sadly, even the counterfeit is exciting to those who have never tasted the real. I remember going on that ride and the sorrow and pain I felt for the people, to be paying to see a cheap imitation.

I am convinced that something very similar is happening in the Church. Whatever is rampant in the culture at large, permeates the church. It smacks of something I once saw on an old Chevy Chase movie, where Chevy found himself entangled in this pseudo religious scene, at a place called Bibleland. Unbelievably, there was a lot of good social comment for religious people in that old movie. I have been all over the USA and other western nations, and what I have seen amongst some ministers and churches, almost made that movie look like a documentary.

Wood Hay and Stubble or Gold?

In 1990 I was visiting Manhattan Beach, in Los Angeles. As I walked along the beachfront area I became aware of a profound presence of the Holy Spirit. God began to speak to me about the state of the church. This awesome indescribable peace just flooded me like a wave.

Phil 4:7 And the peace of God, which passeth all understanding, shall keep your hearts and minds through Christ Jesus. (KJV)

As Gods peace washed over me, He started impressing my spirit about the pseudo religious culture that had infiltrated the church. He impressed upon me that over 90% of all that goes on in some churches has absolutely nothing to do with Him and it was powerless to touch the unsaved. He made it clear that He was using the church anyway but that over 90% of activity was just "pseudo religious activity" and that He had nothing to do with it.

I can almost hear many exclaiming at this point, "Come on Bro. Paul, you can't be seriously saying that over 90% of many church programs are just wood, hay and stubble." All I can say is that is what I believe I heard the Holy Spirit say to me. I am not saying my programs would be the answer, we are all in this boat together and no one can come along and say they are Gods 100% pure oracle of unadulterated truth with the only "Word of Power for the hour". What this speaks to me is that oftentimes mans best attempts to minister for God, are only 10% in the Spirit. God spoke to my heart that day and said in spite of our weakness, failure and immaturity, that the church is still His chosen instrument to reach the world. We are earthen vessels struggling to minister His Gold, Silver and Precious stones; God is using us in spite of ourselves and our failures.

2 COR 4: 7 But we have this treasure in earthen vessels, that the excellency of the power may be of God, and not of us. (KJV)

1 Corinthians 3:11 For no man can lay a foundation other than the one which is laid, which is Jesus Christ. 12 Now if any man builds on the foundation with gold, silver, [a]precious stones, wood, hay, straw, 13 each man's work will become evident; for the day will show it because it is *to be* revealed with fire, and the fire itself will test [b]the quality of each man's work. 14 If any man's work which he has built on it remains, he will receive a reward. 15 If any

man's work is burned up, he will suffer loss; but he himself will be saved, yet so as through fire. (NASB)

God showed me that day, that He is using us not because we are so well trained and awesome but that he is using us to show His Strength, even in our weakness. The amazing thing to me is that he can use our feeble often dysfunctional attempts, to bring Salvation and Healing to the world. No amount of stage set Christianity (sorry, I mean religiosity) is ever going to bring true spiritual freedom. Sure, event oriented religion, can be exciting but anonymous, public, mass, religious activities cannot satisfy the heart cry for intimate communication, friendship and relationship.

Back in 1998, I went to a major men's convention in a local baseball stadium. There were about 30,000 men there and it was a big event. I had, at that time my 11 year old son with me. The feeling of anonymity and blurred facelessness we experienced produced a sense of profound loneliness and expendability. (This group, to their credit, does have smaller home meetings to address the need for relationship.) By and large though, most men only experience the mass production public spectacle, which of course looks great on the TV news. I want to make it clear at this point that I am not against large gatherings and big events for Jesus. The point I am trying to make, is that there is something that is vital, to our spiritual, mental/emotional and even physical health missing from our culture and churches. The laws of physics make irrevocable demonstration of the fact that the macrocosmic cannot exist without the microcosmic.

I have also thought that the ministry team in many large churches are the only ones really having deep fellowship and interaction, hence the team have a very exciting fulfilling church experience. The problem is the average, sheep, congregant or visitor is left watching a big event and marveling at how wonderful the ministry team is but they often feel they are just ordinary people, some feel they are "spiritual losers" that could never be part of the "A" Team. So it is like the crowd at the baseball match that loves the players but never think they could be worthy of actually playing. I left a big church one day like this and I felt very discouraged by the experience, even though it was an awesome church with stellar worship and preaching etc. I felt like an anonymous loser, even though I know the Word of God and I know I can't be a loser in Christ. I went home and read the Bible and had loving fellowship with friends and was restored.

Chapter 17

A DUMMY ISNT A REAL PERSON

One does not have to be a rocket scientist to work out that a dummy is not a living body. It may look like a body, be shaped like a body, and even have clothing like a living body. It is even possible to have a dummy sit in the seat next to you, so you can fool a highway patrolman to enable you to travel in the diamond lane on the CA freeways. (Often we think numbers of bodies in seats make a big church, but they may just be religious dummies, so to speak, not really alive in God yet) A living human body is a macrocosm, made up of a vast microcosmic network of atoms, cells, tissue, bone, muscle and organs which are incredibly and intimately in relationship with one another. The relationship of the microcosmic is what makes life and sense of the macrocosm. One bullet hole in the macro that disrupts vital microcosmic joints such as heart or brain tissue can bring instant death to the whole body.

Many times we blame the devil for our woes, deficiencies and problems but in reality it is most times our own ignorance, laziness or stupidity. The American/Western church today blames many situations and circumstances on Satan. In reality, lots of problems with others could be solved by relationship. The enemy, or those we are in conflict with, is oftentimes created by enmity and alienation, both of these conditions could dramatically improve with dialogue and relationship. If Catholic and Protestant leaders spent time in fellowship more often there would probably be much more unity of the Spirit in the Body of Christ

In days past, I have had the experience of being in contact with

Christians, who have correctly discerned a problem, error, or lack in the church but they have created a bigger problem, by reacting in an extreme self righteous and religious spirit. This spirit has created many errors in church history. I believe one of the biggest needs in the church, is for Christians to get real with each other and this is particularly true amongst the clergy more than anywhere else. Ministers are many times so busy "looking good," and cultivating the appearance of success and church growth to one another, that they are robbed of the awesome and essential blessing, of true open hearted fellowship.

This is not an easy problem to solve, some have attempted to address the issue with the over reaction of a "let it all hang out" session. In this scenario, people go overboard with a "confession session," to the wrong people and their honesty is oftentimes used as a weapon against them. This caused one seasoned ministerial veteran, to warn a junior associate of this kind of foolish transparency with the following advice. He said "If you have anything to confess to anybody, go and find a jackrabbit, confess all of the innermost problems of your life to him and then shoot the rabbit". I know that sounds funny but the lesson is, it is better to confess to the jackrabbit, and then just blather your heart out to anyone who will listen. (i.e. unless you want your laundry on the front page of the church bulletin)

I heard a famous televangelist say after his televised "fall," that one of the biggest needs in his life, was some close friends in the ministry. He said he felt he had reached a place of fame, where he felt unable to just relax and be friends and open up to other ministers. The saying "It's lonely at the top" is truer than we realize. The loneliness at the "top" of ministry notoriety, can be one of the great weapons of Satan to cause a fall.

1 Cor10:12 Wherefore let him that thinketh he standeth take heed lest he fall. (KJV)

Real friendship and transparency in the ministry, is a precious commodity but again it must be real. It is in many ways better to keep your distance and keep your own counsel, than to have fake "religious sincerity and openness". One famous evangelist shared how another "older," (chronologically but not necessarily spiritually) preacher had called him in patronizing tones and announced that he desired to be the younger mans "father". I know that sure does sound "spiritual" and "deep" but that kind of thing, unless it is born of the Spirit, out of years of deep relationship, is the height of religious "hogwash". The older man was more than likely looking for the notoriety, of being the famous younger mans "Spiritual father" in the Lord. This would enhance the older ones delusional egocentric concept of his own authority. Fortunately the wise younger preacher saw through the religious smoke screen and said "Sorry, the job is already taken I already have a real father" and then he mentioned his biological /earthly and true spiritual fathers name.

Oftentimes, men see a need and seek to meet it by legislating an answer, by creating titles and a frame work. The only problem is that titles don't meet the need, only God ordained and anointed relationships do. Also a framework is a far cry from a real building. I have found that the real fathers in the Lord, don't make a great hoo-ha and hullabaloo about being some ones father in Christ, they just do the job and leave the recognition of it to the one being fathered or mentored. The same goes for apostleship, in my experience the real apostles and prophets don't go around putting posters up billing themselves as Apostle Smith or Prophet Jones. Many of the ones I have seen calling themselves Apostle So and So, are some of the biggest Pharisees on the planet, from my perspective.

43 Woe unto you, Pharisees! for ye love the uppermost seats in the synagogues, and greetings in the markets.

44 Woe unto you, scribes and Pharisees, hypocrites! for ye are as graves which appear not, and the men that walk over them are not aware of them. (Luke 11:43 & 44. (KJV)

A man may be a spiritual father to another minister and not even have a ministry nearly as big. The father of the US President does not have to have a more powerful position than his son to be and have been a good father. A true father is pleased to see his son be more successful and honored than himself. A real father is not in need of self trumpeting something like "Listen TV cameras, the only reason my son is successful is because of me, I take full credit and honor and I want the world to honor me." A true father's heart is more than honored to take an obscure public role, with the quiet confidence and joy of knowing that they have been a true Dad to their son or daughter". The real spiritual Dads operate the same way.

It is time for the genuine; the day of the big religious hype of making a public show, is over. I believe that kind of thing grieves the Spirit of Grace. I know it does me. Many ministers want to make a "big Thing" about being "fathers," about being heavy into "family" but their motivation is the good "spin" it will have for their images. Some others, really convince themselves they are into the "deep, sincere" realms of "true" family Christianity but fall prey to the pseudo pious saint routine, you can almost see them polishing their halos and hear them clucking their tongues at the ones not of their "one true" camp. This produces a mealy mouthed brand of religion that is a billion light years from the true spirit of New Testament Righteousness. Yet, others are really using their doctrines, to promote their particular political party or beliefs. Of course they are experts at just the right degree of spin, to make it seem that their brand of "family values" is the only truly spiritual kind. Nevertheless, I am the first to acknowledge that God indeed uses all these flawed ministries, (including me) to preach Christ. As St Paul magnanimously stated all those centuries ago.:

PHILLIPIANS 1:15 Some indeed preach Christ even of envy and strife; and some also of good will:

16 The one preach Christ of contention, not sincerely, supposing to add affliction to my bonds:

17 But the other of love, knowing that I am set for the defence of the gospel.

18 What then? notwithstanding, every way, whether in pretence, or in truth, Christ is preached; and I therein do rejoice, yea, and will rejoice. (KJV)

St Paul was basically saying that some are the real deal and preach Christ in love and humble truth and others are motivated by spiritual baloney BUT.... the bottom line is Christ is preached and Paul was rejoicing about that.

Chapter 18

WEIRD RELIGIOUS SUBCULTURES

Still, one of the greatest needs in the ministry and church today, is reality of relationship and lifestyle. I have often wondered why some of the preachers on television, seem to be part of a strange subculture where really weird fashion statements are rampant. (I fully realize that some of these are wonderful folks, with a great heart for the lost and broken and they truly serve God.) I don't believe God is against being fashion conscious within the realm of good taste and reason but when this eccentric glitzy spirit that borders on masquerade is projected, it can be downright bizarre. It seems to me that some of those ministries have gone over the top.

Note: There is an internationally known, high profile lady minister who I won't name, (some might think I'm critiquing her) she has a very flamboyant hairstyle etc. This lady is a true missionary evangelist/ stateswoman to the world. She has done a vast work of Grace in the Kingdom of God and she is entitled to wear any hairstyle she chooses, as far as I'm concerned. The fruit of her ministry is earth shaking. God bless her forever. I totally exclude her and her people from this sector I'm describing. Many will know who I'm talking about. God uses radical artists and peculiar folks, I know, I'm pretty weird by many people's standards.

Many people are not lacking discernment in regard to some ministers though; they find that this external manifestation of aberrant fashion etc, distracts them and closes their ears to their sometimes wonderful message of Jesus. Please let me attempt to explain. The best statement by the world about this was again made by Chevy Chase when he dressed as a healing evangelist on "Fletch". He appears with this crazy hairdo and suit and has this unbelievable whacky religious demeanor. He is depicted acting out the worst stereotype of an evangelist in action, pushing people over and claiming it was Gods Power etc.

Many people are often dubious when preachers fashion themselves strangely. It would be alright if it was Christian comedy but many are not doing comedy, they are serious. Some seem to think it is really classy and cool to be whacko. Yes, it's true that God looks only at the heart but He is the only one that does. The bottom line is, ministers would be anointed if they preached in Speedos or bikinis at church but they would almost certainly be a stumbingblock, to many they were trying to reach. The dress code can shout so loudly that the message by the preacher cannot be heard by the hearers.

Many of these circus style preachers really huff and puff and gyrate, while screaming very loudly and weirdly, as if to imply it signifies they are anointed. This along with eccentric clothing and mannerisms signifies being unbalanced to a lot of folks. (On the other hand, there are some awesome ministries, particularly the top African American preachers, who truly are anointed and eloquent in the Spirit, when they use lots of emotion and sermon singing with B3 organs etc). One real life evangelist in Australia reportedly hit someone so hard when "laying hands" on a man that he chipped his tooth. Also, once I was in a church in Northern California and a couple who were visiting the church, who looked very well dressed and dignified (one was a professor and one a therapist) suddenly started acting really strangely, they were claiming to be "prophetic chickens" and they were flapping their arms and clucking etc. These people were not kidding either. What craziness to behold. One preacher said, "If they act and sound like animals they should be kept in the zoo."

Sadly, many preachers are really trapped in these stereo types. These cultural and ministerial rituals are as far from God as can be imaginable. I went to a minister's fellowship in one of the USA southern states in the early 90s and it was like being on the stage set of "Fletch lives". Many of the pastors had really strange hairdos and toupees etc and they were acting like parody characters in a comedy sketch, except they were serious. I realize though, that if you were raised in that culture it would seem normal to you. I was fresh from down under in Australia and it seemed ludicrous, compared to my culture. They probably thought I was a weird Australian though, who knows. I know that a lot of those men have great hearts and love God; it was such a strange cultural experience for me and was a stumbling block. On the other hand, I remember one conservative preacher tell how he thought he was at a Rock Concert when he was asked to preach at a big church in Australia. His wife was shocked also; she said the women looked like they were all gyrating in skimpy clothing that she thought was much too revealing for church. The old school preacher also said he thought that drinking wine and beer seemed too prevalent as well.

Ephesians 5:18-20 (MSG)

¹⁸⁻²⁰ Don't drink too much wine. That cheapens your life. Drink the Spirit of God, huge draughts of him. Sing hymns instead of drinking songs! Sing songs from your heart to Christ. Sing praises over everything, any excuse for a song to God the Father in the name of our Master, Jesus Christ.

Personally I don't drink at all, not because I'm trying to be holier than thou, the main reason is that I felt the Holy Spirit told me not too. I also came out of the whole drug scene where alcohol was just another buzz in the drug pantheon. Also alcohol and drug abuse is so interrelated these days that they are all part of the one addiction problem. I recall seeing Eric Clapton tell Larry King how he thought he had given up drugs by switching from cocaine and heroin, to beer and vodka. Eric told how he realized he had not given up anything, he said he just switched addiction vehicles. Of course, Eric has been totally clean and sober for decades now. I find his story and book very inspiring and appreciate his mature attitude to the addiction problem.

These days when people (particularly show biz folks) say they have "a drinking problem", they usually mean they have an all round addiction problem to everything from alcohol, heroin, cocaine, marijuana, ecstasy and tranquilizers etc. It seems to me that in this modern addictive culture, it is unwise for Christians to be proud to say they have the faith to drink wine etc. Even if it is not a problem for the Christian who drinks wine, it may be an influence on someone else that destroys them. I remember a famous Australian pastor telling how he had a glass of wine many years ago on a commercial flight. He didn't know there was a man who had a past of alcohol problems on the flight, who saw him drink his wine. This man hadn't drank in years and he was influenced to drink again, as he reasoned that "If it's good enough for the preacher its good enough for me." Tragically his life was again ensnared by destructive addiction. When the pastor heard the story, he was smitten with deep conviction and resolved to stop drinking wine. He was very upset that his example had such a profound influence on this man.

Romans 14:21b (AMP)

²¹ drink no wine [at all], or [do anything else] if it makes your brother stumble *or* hurts his conscience *or* offends or weakens him.

My wife and I went out to dinner with another minister and his wife back in the mid 1980s. The minister's wife said with a touch of sarcasm that I was way too "holy" to have some wine with them and that I was under the law. I said that I drank the new wine of the Holy Spirit now and that I got the most high with the Most High and I didn't want alcohol as it would not bless me. I was criticized for not drinking, how weird and off base is that? Any body can drink alcohol, it's easy, and it takes no discipline at all. Anyway, the pastor's wife got so tipsy she spilt wine all down her blouse and took it off in public and was walking around in her bra looking for somewhere to wash her blouse in a sink. Her "liberty" doctrine seemed a bit out of hand at that point. They are great people though and we still love them and believe that God will use them. Hopefully, they have adjusted that drinking behavior though. The reality is, the Joy of the Lord is much more fun than being under the influence of wine or any other substance.

Galatians 5:13 (AMP)

¹³ For you, brethren, were [indeed] called to freedom; only [do not let your] freedom be an incentive to your flesh *and* an opportunity *or* excuse [for selfishness], but through love you should serve one another.

I know some of you reading this book may be thinking I'm off target on this point. Well, I have been checking my own heart and attitude and I believe that these things need to be said. We all need constant deliverance from empty or weird religious traditions in order that we might have true relationship in Christ, which is relating in the anointing. Pseudo religion is the mortal enemy of anointing and anointed relationship in the anointing. I came to Christ not to find religion, weird fashions and traditions but real life and love in friendship with God and man. Thank God. Prior to salvation I was a rebel, rock and roll radical. I am still constantly amazed 39 years later (as of 2013--but most of this book was written in 1998-- the earlier testimony section was written in 1991) that I actually became a Christian and even more amazed that I have been a minister of the Gospel for 35 of those years. It is akin to water walking. When I look back over more than thirty five years of walking with Jesus, I am amazed that I have felt satisfied without dosing myself to oblivion with drugs, booze and rock and roll life style.

Before salvation, my first priority of the day was to whack myself with some substance, so that I was "comfortably numb" and unable to feel the terrible pain of living. Drugs place one in a chemically induced vacuum and take away "for a few brief hours" the gnawing lusts, anxieties and tormenting fears that afflict many. I heard someone say that while they provide no answers to life's problems, they often make one forget what the question was. The problem (as it is with all sin) is that after the effects wear off, the problems you are trying to escape return compounded and now you have an addiction, as well as withdrawal pains. This is just as true with the legal prescription drugs like painkillers and tranquilizers (as popularized by the old rock song "Mothers Little Helper." Doctors today are only just beginning to realize the dangers of addiction with many of these short term prescription "fixes". I read recently that far more people died in a recent year of prescription painkillers like oxycodone than from heroin and cocaine combined. The toll for just a year was 39,000 dead which exceeded the national road death toll. Many mixed a couple of drinks with a couple of pills and stopped breathing in their sleep. Many were not even true addicts; they were usually young people having a party. It happened to a young 23 year old girl we knew well, who was a brilliant medical student. She was studying to be a pediatrician and wanted to help kids in third world countries with medical missions. She had never used drugs before but was under peer pressure at a party.

Tangible Tranquility

When Jesus Christ entered my life He literally "INFUSED ME" with awesome doses of love, peace and joy. This was not just some theoretical theological concept, this was real, and it was "tangible," just as real and tangible as a massive rush of sensual pleasure. The song "Jesus on the mainline" has a very close place in my heart because when Jesus rushed into me in 1970s it was awesome. I was in a titanic spiritual battle, I was without hope and without God and without even thinking about it I cried the Name of "Jesus" with every fibre of my being. Instantly, I felt like rivers of liquid light and love just flooded through me with endless waves of healing, cleansing, joy and peace.

Rom 10:13 For whosoever shall call upon the name of the Lord shall be saved.

John 7:38 He that believeth on me, as the scripture hath said, out of his belly shall flow rivers of living water. KJV

39 But this spake he of the Spirit, (KJV)

On another occasion in 1977, I was again under profound spiritual attack and Satan had convinced me that I was no longer able to be delivered. At a point of deep despair, I heard an inner voice more real than any human voice, that penetrated to the very innermost core of my being, it said "I have given you authority over all this" (meaning my despair oppression and bondage) I instantly recognized the voice as being Jesus, some of you are saying "How do you know it was Jesus?" Well, I recognized His voice just like you recognize your wife's voice. Also He was speaking Scripture, which is our greatest Guide, along with The Holy Spirit.

Luke 10:19 Behold, I give unto you power to tread on serpents and scorpions, and over all the power of the enemy: and nothing shall by any means hurt you. (KJV)

John 10: 27 My sheep hear my voice, and I know them, and they follow me:

28 And I give unto them eternal life; and they shall never perish, neither shall any man pluck them out of my hand. (KJV)

When those words were spoken, they were like instant fire in my bones and spirit. The authority of God rose up in me like a consuming fire and I just started saying "JESUS, JESUS, JESUS." Every time I said Jesus, it was literally like a nuclear device exploding in the spiritual realm. I became aware of a dark cloud filled with gargoyle like faces looking at me. As I said "Jesus" the cloud and faces would back up about a small distance. Each time I said Jesus, I became aware that I was delivering massive, insurmountable and devastating blows to this oppressive host. After a number of times just speaking that Name, the cloud of darkness backed right out the door. The second the dark cloud exited, an awesome cloud of Glory (Shekinah Glory) filled the house and a glorious fog, or mist, permeated the atmosphere of the little shack we were staying in. This encounter with the Glory cloud is beyond human ability to adequately describe.

The instant that Holy Fog filled the room, I was instantaneously flooded with "joy unspeakable and full of glory:" 1 Pet1:8b. In that moment I knew, that I knew, that I knew, I had authority over all the power of the enemy (devil). I became aware of the sound of weeping, it was my two friends, a young man and woman both about 20 years of age. They had been with me throughout this ordeal and I had started shouting the Name of Jesus so loud you could hear me 10 miles away. They thought I was losing my mind but now the cloud that was filling the shack touched them so powerfully, that they were on their knees, weeping tears of repentance and calling on the Name of Jesus. It was awesome, they had gotten gloriously saved. We all knelt together renouncing drugs and dedicating our lives to the service of Christ, It was supernatural.

Jesus in Byron Shire---Reprise

The encounter I had that night, was part of a great Holy Spirit move that swept the entire region where I lived. Hundreds of drug users, hippies, musicians, occultists and surfers were saved and there were only a few thousand people in this area, so a few hundred saved in a short period of time was awesome. (Thousands more were powerfully impacted as they traveled through) One of the great trademarks of this move, was it was obviously all God and had absolutely nothing to do with man or church or religious organizations, in the sense that there was no big name preacher came in and no denomination or movement could take the credit. Even though there was no church involved in instigating this revival, amazingly, a number of churches were born from it, some directly, some indirectly. This was a move of God, not a move of religious organizations. Using modern marketing techniques, it is entirely possible to build a large religious movement, out of sheer human organizational ability. Just because a religion or sect has large numbers and media exposure, this in no way ensures validity of Divine origins. Some modern cults have large gatherings and exposure; this does not prove that these aberrant movements are of God.

Once when I was wondering why our ministry seemed so small and inconsequential, compared to many others, the Lord gave me an analogy. He said to me "Just because McDonalds or Burger King sell more burgers than anybody else does not mean that they make the tastiest most nutritious hamburgers. The best hamburgers are often made by small independent operators who are only known in their own neighborhood," God showed me through this statement that just because ones ministry is small and seemingly inconsequential in comparison to huge mega churches and TV ministries, this does not mean that the big high exposure preachers are better, or even more anointed than a smaller one . In fact, it is possible, that like the small hamburger man a small ministry may actually be, in some cases, more excellent than a big one. Oftentimes, the only reason a ministry is big is because of great administration, organization and exposure to a large crowds. It is not because the preaching or ministry is necessarily better than a smaller ministry. Ministers of all magnitudes when it comes to crowd size should encourage themselves with the reality that their ministry is valid and quite possibly as good as or better than the "big names." Religious culture is not a representation of God; rather it reflects unusual local and religious cultural traditions. Sadly many are forced to conform to these non essential aspects, prescribed by church leaders or denominational formulas.

Chapter 19

COOKIE CUTTER CLONE

This in turn breeds the cloning, or cookie cutter syndrome, that is so prevalent. Many have dropped out of fellowship because of these silly traditions. Many have not run from Jesus but have run from aberrant cultural patterns. Of course this situation is encountered in every group of people everywhere but it ought not to be a stumbling block in the Body of Christ. Leaders should be mature enough to not be legalistic about these non essential things. We are called to be all things to all men. We are not called to emphasize our religious or cultural bias. We all have them but must be able to climb above these clouds that obscure the view of the Glorious Light of The Gospel.

Many today want to shine the inglorious light of their tradition, and carry a big cloning cookie cutter, if you don't fit their pattern you are a rebel, a weirdo, or even a heretic. This spirit was encountered by Paul amongst the Judaizers; their cookie cutter was a literal knife to circumcise the foreskin. (Man, that was scary, I'm glad I wasn't in that town) Their attitude was my way or the highway. Cookie cutters always lead to bondage rather than freedom. Whether the legalists want to cut your culture or your anatomy, it is not the true Gospel. The real Gospel is beyond and above religious cultures that arise at different times and locations. The Gospel is the same whether the person preaching it is wearing elaborate clerical robes with a 2 foot long Gold Cross around their neck, or even if the preacher is dressed in swim shorts.

Saddhu Sundar Singh a storied convert from Hinduism, decided to take off his western preachers suit he was told to wear at his seminary and wear his old yellow saddhu robe. His ministry became far more successful to harvest souls in India.

He said God showed him that the people didn't trust someone dressed in western clothing but identified culturally with the yellow robe of the Indian Saddhus. Its similar with the hippies of the Jesus movement in the 1970s, their hairstyles and dress were radically different to the strait laced fashions of the mainline churches, yet the same Gospel worked mightily to save and deliver the hippies who trusted Jesus as Lord. We must all remember that God looks upon the heart, not the external of a person. (I suppose it must also be noted when applying for a new job, that God does look upon the heart but he is the only one that does, so wearing pajamas to the interview is probably not smart)

Thank you for reading this publication, there are many more volumes that could be written, concerning even the revival in Australia's Byron Shire in the 70s and early 80s, let alone the macro vision of the revival that is taking place worldwide as I write this ending May 2013. This reminds me of a wonderful Scripture which I will include as the Final Word

John 21:25[25] And there are also many other things which Jesus did, which if they *were written in detail, I suppose that even the world itself *would not contain the books that *would be written. (NASB)